Risk-Shaped Preaching
Preaching Outside the Box

Terry Biddington

Resource Publications, Inc.
San Jose, California
rpinet.com

©2013 Resource Publications, Inc. All rights reserved. No part of this book may be photocopied or otherwise reproduced without permission from the publisher. For reprint permission contact:

Reprint Department
Resource Publications, Inc.
5369 Camden Avenue, Suite 260
San Jose, CA 95124
408-286-8505
408-287-8748 fax
www.rpinet.com

ISBN 978-0-89390-758-7

Library of Congress Control Number: 2013957610

Printed in the United States of America
13 14 15 16 17 | 5 4 3 2 1

Design: Labour&Play ltd Reg UK7805868
Illustration: Pink Paper Circus

Scripture Quotations from *The New Revised Standard Version (Anglicized Edition)*, copyright 1989,1995 by the Division of Christian Education of the National Council of the Churches of Christ in the United States of America. Used by permission. All rights reserved.

List of Sermons and Biblical texts

Winter

- 8 Winter's Shrouded Silence
  Luke 21:25-36

- 12 New Birth Day
  Isaiah 60:1-6; Matthew 2:1-12

- 16 Rising from the Water
  Luke 3:15-18

- 20 Fig Tree Dreaming
  Micah 4:1-4; John 1:42-53

- 24 Sunflowers Nodding in the Sun
  Malachi 3:1-5; Luke 2:22-40

- 29 Lakeside Sermon
  Luke 5:1-11

- 34 Deadly Nightshade
  Matthew 4:1-11

Spring

- 39 Could I Ask You a Question?
  Matthew 19:27-30; Acts 9:1-22

- 44 A Spot of Bother
  Exodus 17:1-7; John 4:5-42

- 49 Drinking Deep
  1 Kings 18; 2 Kings 4; John 2:1-11

- 54 The Dust of Glory
  John 13:31-35

- 58 The Great Queen's Treasurer
  Acts 8:26-40; John 15:1-8

Summer

- 64 Poolside
  John 5:1-9

- 69 The Holy Spirit Who Beggars Belief
  Acts 2:1-21; John 14:9-17

- 73 On the Road Again
  Acts 2:1-21; John 20:19-23

- 77 Where Do You Go to Find God?
  1 Samuel 15:34—16:13; Mark 4:26-34

- 82 Voices
  1 Kings 19:1-15a; Luke 8:26-39

- 86 Just a Pinch of Revelation
  Exodus 16:13-21; John 6:51-58

- 91 Choosing Life
  Deuteronomy 30:15-19; Luke 10:25-37

- 95 Divine Falsehood
  Ephesians 4:25—5:2

Autumn

- 101 One Day at a Time
  Matthew 16:21-28

- 105 Off the Beaten Track
  Mark 9:30-37

- 109 Just a Couple of Hours
  Luke 16:1-13

- 113 X-rated
  Mark 10:17-31

- 117 The Other Nine Lepers
  Luke 17:11-19

- 121 God's Fireworks
  Revelation 7: 2-4, 7-12; Matthew 5:1-12

- 124 The Algorithm of Salvation
  Isaiah 1:10-18; Luke 19:1-10

- 128 How Many Beans Make Five?
  Luke 3:7-18

Introduction

Sermons go back all the way back to the beginning of the Christian story, and further back still in the Jewish scriptures. But I often wonder whether, if they no longer existed, anyone would re-invent them. Or, more pertinently perhaps, if they do go out of fashion—as they ever threaten to do—whether anyone would actually miss them.

I guess the simple answer is that the sermon form continues to exist because interpretation remains necessary. The interpretation of scripture, of the texts and actions of the liturgy, of the shared experience worshippers have of their spiritual endeavors, and of the collective world view afforded them by their faith. Sermons exist because interpretation is required. This is what the church has always maintained; and the authority of the church is intensely concerned with interpretation.

Not so Jesus, however. He seems rather to have preferred to leave interpretation up to individuals; that is, if they had "ears to hear."

If we're being strictly honest, sermons have often proved somewhat problematic; for the church authorities, for the congregation, and for the preacher. There have, of course, always been helpful aids for preachers, including a medieval Latin collection of sermons aptly titled "Sleep Tight,"[1] for those preachers who struggled to work to deadlines, as well as the great Elizabethan "Book of Homilies,"[2] authorized to be kept in every English church against the sudden absence of the preacher, with its long twenty-five page sermons taking at least an hour each to preach.

Unsurprisingly there has never been any corresponding consideration for those who were expected to endure these long and usually tediously moralizing sermons of yesteryear or, indeed, for those who listen to their (sometimes) shorter cousins of today.

Consequently we have, in so many places, come to have rather low expectations of sermons. Even the word itself, from the French "*sermonner*," meaning to "tell off," is an historic indication of both its anticipated content and of the likely levels of enthusiasm and interest that are all too often generated as the sermon slot in the liturgy draws closer. It seems that few of us really relish the opportunity to listen to a sermon and, except in the case of a few notable popular preachers across the centuries, this has probably always been the case.

This hard reality is incisively summed up by John Shea who writes that sermons are "too often ... only cold coals."[3] They warm no-one's heart, enlighten no one's soul, and excite no one's passion for discipleship or mission. Perhaps I overstate the case. But I suspect not.

I have spent the last ten years or more trying to experiment with sermons and I am grateful that a good number of churches have encouraged me with invitations to preach. If it's possible to reduce their collective feedback to a single phrase often offered to me on my travels, it would have to be: "that was a breath of fresh air!" (But don't forget those generally low expectations!)

Sometimes I have been accused by colleagues of a certain cavalier or else reckless approach to the scriptures. For I like to use the biblical texts as a touchstone for adventures into the borderlands of "what if?", "just suppose," "you'd never believe what happened next," and "surely not!" And this has indeed occasionally led to requests from congregational members to "just tell us what the scriptures *mean*, please!" or "how *exactly* we are to apply them to our lives!" At which point I remind folk of Jesus, and his stories, and his "if you have ears to hear ..." Though one

---

[1] Dormite Secure, last published in Antwerp in 1617.
[2] First published in 1562 and reprinted as Homilies, London: SPCK, 1938.
[3] John Shea, Gospel Light, New York: Crossroad Publishing:, 1998, p. 11.

lay minister was adamant with me: "thanks for coming, but if you come again, do you mind not preaching the gospel. It upsets us!"

Whatever sermons may have been in the past, whatever function they may have served, we are in a very different place today. In large part this is due to the impact of interactive educational techniques, media "sound biting," and the changed way in which we access information. We have become nibblers, grazers, and browsers. We prefer easily digestible (or predigested!) food. And fewer of us than ever before are willing to tackle anything more substantial: anything chunky, tough, chewy, and with much "slower release energy." Most of us prefer instant-fix and sermon-lite!

And, of course, many preachers are more than happy to oblige. Especially given their weekday busyness, lack of time to read, pray, or dream, and the speed at which Saturday night comes round again, already!

So what are sermons for?
At the forefront of my thinking about sermons—as I preach them, help others to preach, and of course listen to preachers in action—has been the idea that they both occupy and create what the Scottish poet Don Paterson calls "the space between us."[4] They *occupy* a particular space in the worship: different perhaps according to religion, religious denomination, or indeed each specific liturgy. But they also *create* a space: a space for listening and hearing, a space for speaking and thinking aloud, a space for dreaming and imagining "what-if?"; a creative-regenerative space in which the Spirit can operate. A space that is *between*:

- the preacher and the congregation
- the preacher, the congregation, and the text
- the gathered community and God
- the present moment and the past, the future, and all eternity

I always try to make the "sermon space" a welcome opportunity for collective lingering: an invitation to take a sideways glance, a seeing out-of-the-corner-of-an-eye, and—perhaps—the occasion to catch a glimpse of something unexpected and potentially life-transforming.

Sometimes I liken the sermon to the "Tardis" of the BBC's time-traveling "Dr Who" TV series: an old-fashioned British police telephone box that is, at the same time, really something quite unexpected. For one thing it is substantially bigger on the inside than it appears from the outside; and for another, it serves a completely different purpose to the one people anticipate. So I offer the sermon as a space for pondering, for dreaming, for imagining alternatives, for scanning distant horizons, or for looking at ordinary mundane things close-up and in real detail. And, of course, for traveling backwards and forwards in time; for making the connections between "back-then Bible time" (which most of us feel we can safely ignore) and the challenges of discipleship in the "here and now" (which many of us prefer not to face).

My task is to attempt to coax people into a liminal space—out through an overgrown or forgotten "back door way" in their souls, hearts, and minds—where they might encounter (or, more accurately, be encountered by) the living Spirit of God. I try to get under people's skin to make them itch and so begin to scratch their minds and souls. I work at opening up a chink in their spiritual armor, their liturgical ennui, and their prosaic (prose-ache!) boredom with the routine repetition of over-familiar biblical texts. I push at the established and accepted norms of sermon form and

---

[4] A line from his poem "The Day," in Rain, London: Faber and Faber, 2009, p. 41.

content, and at the expected modes of sermon listening and hearing, to see what might be created and communicated; to see what might happen next.

Sometimes nothing happens and the congregation's time-worn end-of-worship greeting: "nice sermon, vicar!" occurs as it will have done there during all living human memory. Sometimes nothing happens because what they hear is so totally outside received expectations that it goes unrecognized as "sermon." (One colleague told me confidently that I had "failed to communicate anything!") And so I have learned that when I visit a "new" church, I have to prepare the congregation for "something unusual from your visiting preacher today." (The knowledge that I work with students is usually taken as the excuse for my unusual approach!) Sometimes too, particularly when training new preachers, there's the suggestion that I demand too much from listeners: "You seem to expect the congregation to do all the thinking." Well, yes, I think I do actually expect them to engage; but I'm also very happy if they want to use the space to sleep or day dream. That may be just the opportunity the Spirit wants or their bodies need!

Very often though, what happens is that during the sermon (and sometimes too in the silence immediately afterwards) we—preacher and congregation, individually or together—find ourselves in unexplored territory, somewhere beyond our preconceived or erstwhile accepted understandings, and "on the edge of a precipice (Shea, 1998, 48)." Or else we discover ourselves at a place of conceptual breakthrough, at a moment of epiphany or (wonderful phrase) "curiosity startle,"[5] and so, at a place for taking a deep breath and saying "yes" to the mysterious, enticing, calling of the Spirit.

What I consciously aim to do is to bring (charm, coax, cajole, tempt, or seduce) the congregation into an immediate and inescapable encounter with the scriptural text. For, all too often, scripture (by virtue of it being "in the Bible") has hugely less relevance to us that anything we might read in the press or in some celebrity magazine. So some creative-cunning is necessary to engage them. Often too, many people prefer to "reify" or objectify the scriptures: to think things *about them*, rather than letting the Word and Spirit behind and within the text interrogate *them*, entice *them* out of their box, and lead *them* to rearrange their own mental furniture, in the very way that music, art, stories, poetry (and good counseling?) seek to do.

Consequently I deliberately explore the relationality between words and texts "midrashically." I do this by juxtaposing and contraposing the texts themselves, the congregation and the texts, the "back then" and the "here and now," and by moving backwards and forwards, to and fro, between them all. I also exploit the potential words have for signifying more than one thing at the same time and so try to create a text that is freighted with multiple levels of meaning, in the manner of poetry, instead of following the traditional assumption that the sermon must communicate *the preacher's message*, or else simply "fail." My hope and prayer is that the Spirit will connect with the hearer's imagination and that meaning will emerge from this encounter, at the Spirit's prompting. And as a result people frequently tell me things like: "I'd never thought about it like that," "I've heard that text many times and never understood it," "I like the way you don't impose a meaning on us," "I saw the text in a new light," and "I was carried off inside the story and experienced it afresh."

There is also, from time to time, the charge (largely from fellow clergy) that I use language in a manner that is "too complex for the congregation," or for the "simple believer." Now I find that

---

[5] Daniel Dennett, Breaking the spell: religion as natural phenomenon, New York: Penguin Books, 2006, quoted in Armin W. Geertz "New Atheistic approaches in the cognitive science of religion," in Michael Stausberg ed, Contemporary Theories of Religion, Oxford: Routledge, 2009, 246.

a rather extraordinary and condescending assertion! (I wonder whether anyone says the same to pop singers, performers, song writers, and poets.) I suspect that what they actually mean is that either that the ideas presented are too complex (in which case I suspect that's an indictment against the church's historic failure to communicate theological ideas deemed "too disturbing" for lay folk), or else, as I hinted earlier, that the form is so unlike the traditional sermon that people initially fail to recognize it.

And so to the form
What I'm striving to create is a sermon that has a broadly narrative base line, to give it harmony and structure and to carry the congregation along, together with a series of improvisations "on top." These improvisations may take the form of a short meditation, an excursus, (perhaps a flash back or forward through time), or a playful development of the text, its ideas, or characters. They might also be in the shape of an impromptu time of silence, or music; or else an imagined dialogue. I've also often found it productive to adopt the format of a screenplay and encourage the congregation to imagine a film or movie playing. (Much like the familiar *modus operandi* of the so-called "Ignatian method" of meditation.)

I guess what I'm after is a rich, eclectic, hybrid, and spellbinding format that might be "experienced" as much as "heard." Whatever else I think I'm about, I believe I have very high expectations for what "sermon" might be. And the greatest satisfaction has been those very many occasions when people ask for a copy of the text to take away and study. (Or, these days, download.)

And I always have a written text. I find it impossible to preach in this way without one. Moreover I am completely unable to preach from A4 "portrait" pages of continuously typed prose as I find this detracts too much from a generous eye-contact and fails to allow the text to rise off the page and inhabit the space between preacher and congregation. Consequently I write in very short lines (A4 "landscape") that are able to be caught up from the page, in groups of three or four lines, with only the shortest glance away from the congregation.

What you have before you in this book is very much the text as preached. The most significant change is that I have elided lines and words in an attempt both to give a visual sense of the pauses, spaces, tensions, and anticipations of my delivery, and to make them much slower to read. The overall result is that the format on the page takes as long to read silently and thoughtfully as it does to preach aloud. And you may also try reading the texts out loud.

The point of it all
My intention is three-fold. First I hope that this collection will give encouragement to preachers and would-be preachers to experiment for themselves, in their own ways, and limited only by their own imaginations. On preaching courses I'm often told by colleagues that they could never "preach like that." I know from experience though that they then generally always discover otherwise when they give themselves permission to do so.

Secondly I hope that people will see that it's possible to use fewer words to achieve more: the "Tardis effect." I aim to use roughly one thousand words per sermon and try never to go more than two hundred words over, unless the occasion specifically demands this. Such a word count offers about fifteen to twenty minutes of text and silence.

Introduction

Finally it is my great aspiration that I might persuade those who listen to sermons—do we call them consumers, customers, or cognoscenti?—to engage more proactively with the business of preaching and sermon "reception." Most clergy put a great deal of effort into their preaching and both need and value encouragement, critical comment, and friendly observations. The "nice sermon, vicar" syndrome I mentioned earlier is well intentioned, but—to my mind, at least—"nice" is a pretty meaningless and anodyne compliment.

At the end of the day, the task of improving the standards of preaching and raising expectations about sermons is something that involves all of us. I believe that good, creative, and inspiring preaching has a real future as a radical, alternative, and Spirit-filled way of communication among the people of God. My prayer is that we might all make it part of our Christian ministry and discipleship to encourage and nurture this in our midst, in the service of Jesus Christ, and of the God who continues (in the familiar phrase of Walter Brueggemann) to "utter Easter" and delight us all in the Spirit.

I am grateful to all those congregations who have invited me to preach and especially to the ever enthusiastic members of that extraordinary group of Christians and spiritual seekers at St Peter's House Church and Chaplaincy in the Manchester Higher Education community UK, who are my present companions on the journey of life. I am most deeply honored that Stephen Lowe agreed to provide an Afterword and am grateful to David Ackerman, Una Kroll, Michael Lewis, Michael Wakelin, and Stuart Wild for their encouragement with this project.

Finally I must also express a continuing deep gratitude to Fiona for her illustrations. What I try to do with words, she achieves much more readily and lovingly with the simple tools of her craft and a God-given way of seeing the glory of the world. It is to her that I dedicate this book.

A word about the illustrations
Fiona trained at the Norwich School of Art, UK, where she left with a first class degree in Visual Studies, followed by a Masters Degree in Fine Art from the University of the Arts, London.
For more information, or just to say hello, please go to www.pinkpapercircus.com

Terry Biddington
Feast of the Transfiguration 2010

Luke 21:25-36

WINTER

Branches coming into bud in a winter wood

01 Winter's Shrouded Silence
(Luke 21:25-36)

> "When you see these things taking place you know that the kingdom of God is near."

On Friday I took myself off
to Wales. I walked for miles along the Ceiriog river, west of Chirk. It wasn't my first visit there,
for I've walked those banks before—at the first signs
of the burgeoning of spring, and
in the heat of the summer when the hedgerows are thick with flowers and insects. But

Friday was different. The river was
flowing fast and swollen between almost completely bare trees. The dead
leaves had blown into hollows, cracks, and hedgerows, revealing
things previously hidden from the eye by thick greenery, and so laying them open
to view. There
were the leveled remains of one or two ancient cottages and, higher up
the valley slopes, a wall here and an arch
there: the ruins of slate works of some sort. The vestiges

of whole lives and human toil and
aspiration spent and gone
forever, beyond recovery; generations passed away.

At times the pathway left the river bank behind and rose above it into stretches
of wood. Here the sounds of the river were dulled. The air was colder and silent, save
for the occasional cry of a game bird disturbed by my approach.

And here the paths themselves had evidently been recently cleared. Birch and elder and oak stumps
lined the way, protruding
from the damp earth with, every few yards
neat piles of usable wood, all graded according to size,
or else heaps of tangled branches fit only for the fire. Like old pictures of the torments of hell.

At length I sat on one of these newly cut stumps, all shiny now
in the rain that had begun to fall. I sat and I looked around me.

A subdued palette of colors: the many grays
of the birch and slate, the greens
of the moss and decaying leaves, the browns
of the cut, beringed surface of the wood and the palest rose madder
of an occasional fungus. And there was silence all around me.

After the autumn color and bounty, the winter is a time of great stripping away and laying bare.
Everything cut back to stark outlines of essential shapes and angular skeletons.

01 Winter's Shrouded Silence

Then come the biting cold frosts, killing off what's meant to be gone, purging and cleansing
with its silvery beauty, laying waste the plenty
and casting a cloak of dead brittleness over everything;
reducing even the air to a turgid not-to-be-disturbed stillness.

Winter, like older age, is when all is trimmed back and revealed for what it is—
and for what it has been all along;
a time for discerning God's
ever-presentness, God's
mysterious, gentle, deftness of touch in the half-light grayness of a freezing day.

Above all the winter is a time of watching for signs.
Watching for signs—and waiting.
For what is there to do but sit and watch and wait? Waiting

for an unknown word to be whispered by an unseen voice;
a word that cannot be spoken by mortals—but only heard
a word that speaks a "yes" to the "no" of winter's thrall
a word to penetrate the numbness
a word to resurrect the deadness and bring newness.
A word that, while coming out of silence, can never be reduced to silence
because its full meaning is inexhaustible:
unfathomable to the human mind.
Like a sonata, a love's embrace, a poem, a sunset, a baby's hand, a leaf's frozen skeleton.

A word we need to hear repeated over and over,
but which we can never memorize, capture, fix on paper, or tame in speech.
Like a story—ever different with each telling.

A word to cause a righteous branch to spring forth;
A word to birth a child in the dead brittleness of unrighteous winter
and so make again a child of us.

A word with the power of rebirth,
unforetold by human wisdom or divining.
A word that comes as stealthily as the frost,
as swiftly as a shower of rain
as longed for as the rising of the moon to guide the way.

A word that is light.
Whose coming is indiscernible—save to those able to receive and ready to welcome.
Whose advent—visible only to those who sit in silent contemplation
and embrace the signs of the empty barrenness all around
and learn to read in them their own frail beauty,

their own darkness and certain mortality;
their own smallness and need for loving back to life.

At this time of year
there is nothing to distract us from the need for preparation.
Preparation for what lies ahead;
for deadness and deep silence,
for the purging and cleansing of a long frosty night,
for the anticipation of finding God in the most lifeless of places
and for the assurance of discerning the signs,
like tight, closed buds on a lifeless branch.
Signs that speak of one-day-soon rebirth, and fresh life, color, and scent;
and of the distant
—did you hear it then?
—voice calling.

A voice that calls us back and on and out and up to joy.
A voice that calls us home and bids us enter.
From darkness to light:

For while gentle silence enveloped all things, and night in its swift course was now half gone, your all-powerful word leapt from heaven, from the royal throne,...(Wisdom 18:14f).

Isaiah 60:1-6; Matthew 2:1-12

WIN
TER

Ornithogalum umbellatum
Star of Bethlehem

Galium verum
Lady's Bedstraw

"The flowers of both plants have been likened to the star of the nativity. Whereas the former grows in profusion in the Middle East, there is a legend that the virgin Mary had a mattress made of Lady's Bedstraw because the animals had eaten all the other fodder in the stable."

02 New Birth Day

(Isaiah 60:1-6; Matthew 2:1-12)

Today the prophet Isaiah and the evangelist Matthew announce the arrival of kings coming from the east. Kings or magi: so-called wise men. Or else perhaps star gazers, or jobbing astrologers, or unemployed magicians seeking work.

We know their story off by heart, surely—and the precious gifts: gold, frankincense, and myrrh. Gifts wrapped in layers of meaning.
Gold—to show that the child has been born to be a king.
Frankincense—because he is to be worshipped.
And myrrh—to foretell his suffering.

But suppose, just suppose, that instead of three kings—they'd been three queens.
Or instead of three wise men—three wise women.
Do you think that might have made some kind of difference? Just think about it for a moment.

Instead of following a star—they'd have planned ahead and got themselves a map.
Instead of arriving twelve days *after the birth*—they'd have been there on time. (Or a little early. Thanks to the map.)
And instead of standing around looking as sheepish as the sheep,
they'd have helped Mary with her breathing exercises, and delivered the baby;
fussing over their sister Mary, cleaning the stable, organizing Joseph:
and then making a nourishing casserole with good wine and fresh bread.

And they'd have brought practical gifts too.
(As, surely, any woman knows!)
Like real Peace on Earth from that day forth.

Now all of this set me thinking about the gifts that I'd given over the festive period.
And not just the gifts themselves but *the reasons why* I'd given particular things to particular people.
And the spirit in which I'd given them.
And the manner in which I'd received gifts from my loved ones—especially if they weren't what I'd have chosen myself.
And why it was that I'd perhaps *not given gifts* to some people this year?
And whether perhaps I am a "vengeful giver?"

Giving gifts, shopping for Christmas, birthdays, anniversaries, or weddings is not an easy thing to do. For it captures well how we can often be creatures with very mixed motives. Not
always giving "out of the best of intentions."

Let's consider our own practice for a moment.

Do we start with a particular price or budget in mind for each gift?
Is the price tag the thing?
(Like most of those wedding lists you get these days—where you're encouraged to think of the price and then find a gift.)

If we have lots of relatives, grandchildren, brothers and sisters, friends—do we try and get away with the minimum? Or do we think that we have to spend a fortune before we can feel we've offered a "real" gift? And is there no longer a place for making our own gifts to offer? Do
we get the first thing that comes to mind? Or do

we put lots of thought into the gifts we buy? Walking for hours round the heaving shops. Do we like to "get it all sorted" by October, by the summer, by the previous January's sales? Do we really struggle to find "must-have" gifts for people who already have everything? And do we like to see expressions of joy and surprise on the faces of those we give to?
Are we upset with anything less than obvious deep gratitude on their part?

Now we may recognize ourselves in these caricatures. But
what about the gifts we receive?

Do you know how to fake it—turning feelings of disappointment into expressions of delight?
Can we smile divinely when the paper's torn away to reveal something dreadful?

Do we find it hard to receive gifts? Blushing with embarrassment at a really expensive present? Or when someone knows you intimately enough to give you exactly what you most desire?

Do you long for there to be someone in your life to give you a gift of any sort?
Do we miss the gift of the presence of a loved one no longer with us?
And would one minute spent in their presence mean more than any presents?

Perhaps, though, you are one of those people
old enough and wise enough to know that all that really matters are the simple but important things in life:
the chance to live and love again another day
the chance to start another year in the company of friends
the chance to walk another while in the presence of God.
Perhaps you are blessed enough to know contentment.

But most of us are, in truth, endlessly still searching
for some thing truly, lastingly, meaningful.
Some thing that speaks to us at the deep level of our insecurity
that speaks to our fearfulness.
Some voice that teaches us "do not be afraid."
Some hand in which to put our own.
Some gift that brings us life and joy.
Some treasure never
to be forgotten, lost, or broken. So in this spirit
I offer this small seasonal thought. A take-away thought.
to take home and digest
later. For a private epiphany:

Because we live with the fearful knowledge of our death one day,
we choose to call ourselves "mortals."
We allow our mortality to define and color our whole life and its living.

But
suppose on this Twelfth Night, before we pack away the decorations for another year, we learn a new word. (To scribble on the box, to be found and remembered next time round.)
A new name for ourselves.
And suppose we let the new-born child give us this name.

WIN
TER

A name that is his own strange and magical gift to us.
A name that gives us a fresh way of looking at our lives;
a fresh clue to the fullness of our existence.
A practical Christmas gift that—*for each day of the years to come*—can turn on its head
our preoccupation with our death.
Would that be of any interest to you?

Suppose we let the new-born child himself call us—wait for it; get out those notepads—not "mortals," but "natals." The very opposite!
"Natals." "People of the nativity." His
nativity. People
born to live life without fear of death—because, truly, death is nothing. People
born to encourage self, and each, and all, and others to live life fully
to live life by putting effort into living life
into making caring homes
into building inclusive community
into being involved in society
into breaking down barriers between people
into creating good businesses and great art
into proclaiming again and again the birth of Christ in the world
as if, and
precisely because,
our own births and lives depend on it.

So, natals one and all!
Accustom yourselves to your new name. Try it on. Test it out. Speak it. Live it.

Then return home today—not by "another route," as those first wise men and women did.
But by your usual route! But
let your new-found insight, this small practical gift of take-away wisdom,
allow you to see familiar things differently.

And may we find it in our hearts to thank one small
child at his nativity
for showing us a magical way to new birth, new life, and new living.
For ever, for always, and for sure ...

Luke 3:15-18

WINTER

Iris pseudacorus
Iris

"The Frankish King Clovis adopted the symbol of three yellow irises on his banner after his defeat of the Romans and his consequent conversion to Christianity and baptism."

03 Rising from the Water
(Luke 3:15-18)

There's a tension at the start of the four gospel narratives about what constitutes the beginning of Jesus'
story. Is his beginning to be found in the great birth narratives of Matthew and Luke?
Or at his baptism—with which Mark and John commence their gospel witness?

Was Jesus *born great*—the typical expectation of classical and medieval literature? Or does the vignette
of his baptism rather hint that Jesus grew,
during his formative years, into a special
maturity, and a particular
self-understanding
of his relationship to the creator God?
Does he arrive at a crisis
of spiritual awareness? Does he discover a sense of vocation? And

does all this,
and more,
come together at this one moment, this singularity,
of his baptism? Urging him on
to step forward and join the queue on the river bank? Dizzying him
as he waded out to where John struggled to stand upright?

But fail not to think about the ways in which the Christian tradition has taken the story of Jesus' mature
commitment that day in the Jordan
and built around it a complex web of messages about the need for *spiritual rebirth*
that has
all too frequently
been so emphasized as to deny the importance of our *physical birth*
and to devalue the maternal:
often reducing the mothers who bore us and nurtured us
to the level of those things that "need to be set aside and left
behind"
as we set out on our spiritual journey.

As we set out on our journey. And where exactly? Heavenward? Towards our death?

The short, too-short, space between our birth and death
being the little time we have
to work hard,
to avoid temptation,
to stay on the straight and narrow (—or else!)
to strive to reach that "second birth" of which the carol sings
to live out the promises of *our baptism*
(fighting all the way against sin, the world, and the devil)
so that, at the end, we may save our souls
(*our souls* mind, mine and yours—no need to worry about anyone else's!)
until finally, finally, we "enter into life"? Our *just* reward?

No wonder we call ourselves "mortals";
our lives but a series of reminders of our mortality.
Our politics, economics, ethics, religion—why, even our bodily pleasures—

03 Rising from the Water

being but projections of our preoccupation with our own death and
with our need to deny, survive, and insure against it for as long as possible.
Saving our soul and attaining "real and ever-lasting life"
no matter what the expense; no matter
who else might have to suffer or pay for it.

The story of Jesus of Nazareth at his baptism might just be read another way, though.

As the story of a young man who
born from the flesh of the woman Mary
born into a family, into a network of connections, into a continuum of kinship and ancestors
raised by her and by them
nourished by his awareness of all that bound him,
connected him
viscerally, umbilically,
to that humanity; yet aware,
because of all that connection,
of his own uniqueness as a son of God.

As the story of a young man who,
nervously,
steps out that day for baptism
because he discerns in his being the possibility that his birth and his beginning
—how ever, what ever it was—
was yet a clue to the way life might be lived.

As the story of a young man whose baptism was a first coming-to-fruition of all that had nurtured and
nourished and *mothered* him
empowered him and inspired him
to step out into a public world
of words and signs,
and prophecies of old
of deeds and encounters
with people, hurting.
Hurting because they had lost, forgotten, or been denied *their* connectedness,
because they had been rejected, abjected, subjected,
cut asunder, separated from the body; disconnected:
women, prostitutes, tax collectors,
the mad, the bad, the ill, the lame, the shepherds, the fools, the dying;
those unable to fulfill the righteous demands of legal cleanliness.

As the story of a young man who, because of his birth and his beginning,
because of his nativity—his *natality*—and his coming-to-baptism
because of his awareness of life as potential-to-be-lived-and-offered

was able to show how life might be lived:
not as the selfish, grab-what-you-can-while-you-can, road to mortality …

was able to show how we find our wholeness, our salvation, our eternal life:

WIN
TER

not as an undertaking for ourselves alone ...

was able to show how saving our soul can only be done, only be done, only be done
by embracing the needs and lives of our brothers and sisters, far and wide
and of those too-close for comfort ...

was able to show how faith is not a well-endowed policy or a cast-iron guarantee,
as a down payment on our eternal security,
or even as a warm feeling to keep us snug in the dark times ...

was able to show that faith is a risky business;
unsure, uncertain;
though clearly offered, costly to seize,
and whose living-out is something of a secret:
provisional on our making the connections
between ourselves and those and the world around us;
provisional on us granting to Death only our death
and to living our lives, our potential,
as one beginning, one birth, one plunge of baptism, one coming to fruition,
one flourishing after another ...

And finding therein all that we are called to be.

From this then might flow for us, as church,
an understanding of mission as an *ever bringing to fruition*
as an ever nurturing what is among and around us.

Helping what *already* is to flourish,
bringing to birth what is calling out to be,
celebrating newness and fresh beginnings,
blessing the diversity of the lives around us,
and creating a space
in which the divine spirit may work only as she can.

And bless us even as we seek to bless others.

John 1:42-53

WINTER

Ficus carica
Fig

04 Fig Tree Dreaming

(Micah 4:1-4; John 1:42-53)

> " [God] shall judge between many peoples,
>   and shall arbitrate between strong nations far away;
>   they shall beat their swords into plowshares;
>   and their spears into pruning hooks.
>   nation shall not lift up sword against nation,
>   neither shall they learn war any more;
>   but they shall all sit under their own vines and under their own fig trees,...
>   and no-one shall make them afraid (Micah 4:3-4b)."

It is dangerous to sit under fig trees.
Or any sort of trees really.
But especially fig trees.
As Nathanael discovered to his cost.

Resting after a day's labor in the sun;
resting in the drowsy heat under the tree's shade.
Dozing, sleeping perhaps.
Dreaming—and what a dream!

They shall all sit under their own vines and fig trees. And no-one shall make them afraid.

It was so for Nathanael of Cana
as he sat dozing under his fig tree that day.
The sun was so bright that he lay with his eyes half-closed
enjoying the bliss of the moment.
Wasn't this what Micah's prophecy was all about? he thought.
The prophecy of bliss at the end of all days.

His mind was stilled and his heart was full of good things.
Life wasn't too bad, he murmured to himself as he dozed. And then he was asleep again.
Dreaming of peace and bliss, and harmony; of swords turned into plowshares.

God shall judge between many peoples
and shall arbitrate between strong nations far away.

They shall beat their swords into plowshares
and their spears into pruning hooks;

Nation shall not lift up sword against nation
neither shall they learn war any more.

They shall all sit under their own vines and fig trees.
And no-one shall make them afraid.

It is fascinating to analyze the DNA of dreams.
They are a heady mixture of lived experience and thoughts and memories:

spiced with a pinch of deep-seated anxiety and finished off
with soupçon of unspoken desire.
And Nathanael's was no exception.

His country was little more than a cross roads between the bigger nations around about;
constantly fought over, pillaged, and looted.
And, even as he sleeps, his country was held a hostage to fortune by an invading force,
ruled over by a puppet king installed by the Romans.

So the words of Micah called to him in his dream—as they often did.
Speaking of a time to come;
of swords turned into plowshares
spears into pruning hooks,
and of sleepy fig trees in the sun.
Just a dream—or are such things possible?
Just a dream—or is this the stuff of gritty reality?
Just a dream? Still a dream?

Nathanael dreamed on.
In his dream he hears the cry of daughters sitting beside their dead mothers,
of mothers holding dead sons,
of sons weeping at the funerals of their fathers,
of fathers turning plowshares into weapons,
of fire and screaming and the deafening cries of the wounded and dying,
of fig trees burning in the night.

And then he hears a voice,
from somewhere deep down in his dream,
beyond the noise of war and slaughter.
A voice calling his name.

Nathanael rouses himself from his dream and wipes his brow.
Only a dream, he sighs. But he feels his heart bleeding ...

He shields his eyes with his hand. The sun is a blaze of fire.
And Philip is standing over him breathing hard.
Philip, that old rogue from the tavern, is calling to him:

"Come and see. Come and listen. Wake up!
It's Jesus—the one I mentioned last night. The man from Nazareth.
Yes—Nazareth, of all places, I know.
But come—you'll be amazed."

Philip pulls Nathanael up onto his feet—and down onto the road.
"Come and listen to what he's saying. He has a dream."

By the wall at the edge of the road Jesus turns and looks at him.
Nodding
in apparent recognition.

WIN
TER

Nathanael asks whether they have met before. But already he knows.
"Why I saw you under the fig tree dreaming the dream of Micah.
Come,"
says Jesus. "Follow me. And see greater things still."

And here we are. All this time later.
Here we are—sitting under our own Sunday-best fig trees.
Chilling out after the stresses of the past week; enjoying
a lazy day of rest, a day of peace and quiet
a day for tranquility, a day for dreaming dozily.

What is it that we dream of?
Does anything particular disturb our peaceful sleeping?

Listen awhile—can you hear it?
A voice—whispering somewhere close-by
A voice calling
softly; calling
our name: yours and mine ...
"Come and see. Come and see," it says. "Listen."

A voice that we've heard in our dreams,
but which longs to speak through our lips and in our lives.
A voice to turn our dreams into reality.
If we could bear that.

A voice calling us to wake up and shake off our slumbers;
a voice calling us to follow
a voice we'll find disturbing, fearful, unsettling, unwelcome, demanding
more than we can give.
A voice that will challenge all who think they're sitting securely
under the well-founded fig-tree assumptions about life.

A voice whose action in our own flesh and blood can
scarce be resisted.

A voice urging us to action: to change the world:
swords into plowshares, spears into pruning hooks,
ignorance into truth, truth into justice, justice into peace—real peace, God's peace
shalom!—for everyone.

But
be warned. Be warned. It's so very demanding-dangerous
to sit under fig trees! Even Sunday-best ones!

And if you dare consume this bread and wine today—the dream fades and
the clock of real life starts ticking.
Watch out there!

Malachi 3:1-5; Luke 2:22-40

WIN
TER

Helianthus annuus
Sunflower

05 Sunflowers Nodding in the Courtyard

(Malachi 3:1-5; Luke 2:22-40)

Come rain, come shine they were always there.
Simeon and Anna,
Or—to give them their English names—"Darby and Joan."

Always in the Temple,
hanging about, talking with strangers,
giving guided tours to overseas visitors
in exchange for a few coins to help eke out their pensions ...
Or, who knows?
Perhaps it was mainly to get them out of the house and into the sun.

But faithful they were, day after
day, sabbath after
sabbath, year after
year. Until
now they were so "full of years" that they couldn't exactly remember how long it had been.

Some of you may know what it's like to be Simeon and Anna.
Some of you will have seen dozens of people, and families, and clergy come and go
in this place.
Some of you have seen lots of changes over the years.
And many of you will know how hard and exhausting it is to keep changing and saying yes
to the future.
Even though, in the end, change is the only way of looking to the future.
And Simeon and Anna certainly seem to have struggled too...

Interviewed afterwards by the local paper, Simeon couldn't recall whether this particular day
had begun
any differently. He'd arrived at the Temple at his usual sort of time and stood first
to face the sun, just where it falls inside the east gate. (You probably know the spot I mean.)

He loved to feel the sun's heat on his old bones and on his face. Like a sunflower, he was.
Then he moved to his accustomed place at the foot of the main steps and sat down to watch
the people coming and going. Each one he studied closely,
nodding at them, straining
to read what he could from their dress, or manner of walking, or body language.

And with each new face he remembered how, years before, he'd once had the strangest idea
that if he spent all his remaining days in the Temple precincts, he might be the
very
first
person
in
the
world
to see the face of the Anointed One.
The one who'd come to save Israel from those "so-and-so" Romans! Simeon spat
the word
out of his mouth.

('So-and-so,' you will realize, represents a very rude word in Hebrew.)

And each night, as Simeon went home, people would cry out to him,
in a teasing sort of way: "Any luck today, granddad?"

A figure cut across Simeon's train of thought.
Richly dressed and swaggering, with a bevy of retainers following after him.
A wealthy merchant or a powerful diplomat, perhaps. Perhaps? Perhaps? Perhaps?
Simeon searched his face for a sign. Then: "No. Not him."
And he saw instead another figure, further off. Tall and erudite. A scholar. But: not him, either!
And he moved over into the sunlight again and settled down.

Then Simeon found himself contemplating the impossible.
He suddenly thought that *this*
unexpected figure before him was perhaps the One: for
cannot God
do the impossible?
Doesn't God
move in mysterious ways? Could it be?
His mouth fell open as he realized that this *woman* approaching
might be the One.
He stared at her, long and hard—until she saw him staring, and gestured rudely back.
No. Apparently not her either!

At noon old Anna came out into the sun with her bread.
Simeon nodded towards her.
She knew his game of old, his watching and waiting, watching and waiting.
(And, though many rightly called him prophet, she played it too.)
But today it was a welcome freedom from prayer and prophecy to be out in the hot sun.

She turned to follow his gaze and found a young soldier, strong and very fit.
For a moment his beauty confronted her with
forgotten memories of her own youth, and
stirrings
she thought her body had also long-ago forgotten!
Then she shook herself with laughter and began to eat.

And, so bizarrely,
it was this act of *eating* that ultimately took her mind off *watching*.
And,
(though the Bible fails to mention this),
led to Simeon being indeed the very first person to greet Mary and Joseph and their baby
as they entered the Temple!

"*A baby, of course*," thought the old man; and everything suddenly fell
into place in his mind.
(Though how many other babies had he seen there before, already?
And *this one*: was it a boy—or a girl?) How
he rushed across the square to find out.

WIN
TER

And how his old heart leapt!

"See," prophesied Malachi the messenger,
"See, I am sending my messenger to prepare the way before me,
And the Lord whom you seek will suddenly come into his temple."

Simeon and Anna, Darby and Joan, you and me,
What does it take for us to be able to recognize the Lord "suddenly coming into his temple?"
And do we come to church ever expecting to see such a thing?
To find God in here, rather than outside?
(God sitting on a pillar somewhere—amusing him-herself by flicking
dust
down
onto the preacher?)

Do we come to church expecting to find anything very much at all?
Do you expect anything at all to come of following the Christian way?

For centuries the Jews had longed for a savior. There were all sorts of theories as to what a savior would mean; all kinds of
different expectations
But what do we long for?
What do we expect—of God? of this church? of each other? of ourselves?

Do we expect to find what we've always expected—or have we stopped bothering?
Do you expect to find what you've always expected—or are you prepared to be surprised and delighted, like Anna and Simeon?
Or do we not expect to find anything at all? (Church just being a safe, comfortable, habit.
Something to do on a Sunday morning to while away the time before lunch.)

Might we be more like Anna and Simeon and come expecting the glory of God to be revealed in the temple?
(No, I'm serious!)
The glory of God? The thing that makes God look down and smile?

What is it?
The glory of God: the thing that makes her proud of her handiwork.
The thing that *really* tickles her fancy and makes her slap her metaphorical thigh in delight.

What is it? Can you guess?
The glory of God—wait for it—is a human being, fully alive.
(Watch my lips, please!)
The glory of God—is a human being fully alive.
(Repeat it in your souls: twice daily before meals.)

The glory of God is the fully aliveness to the future-whatever-it-holds
of Simeon and Anna, faithfully rooted to their spot in the sun,
The glory of God is the fully aliveness
of Mary and Joseph, the brand-new parents, as they delighted and wondered at these two old eccentrics,

wizened and dried by the years in the sunshine of keen expectation.
The glory of God is the fully aliveness to-the-future
they felt
even as those fearful prophetic words shivered down their spines.
The glory of God is the fully aliveness
of that small baby (*it was a boy*, by the way)
as it cooed and gurgled and waved its arms in pure excitement at the world and everything in it.
The glory of God is a human being fully alive!

And, remarkably, (yes, remarkably!) it is in fact
for "fully aliveness,"
for rejoicing and celebrating the sheer wonder of being alive in the world,
for letting go of what troubles us and wearies us,
cripples us, and wounds us,
and for celebrating the good news of a victory over death, and a victory *for aliveness*,
remarkably:
it is for this reason alone
that we are called together to be church and called
to share this news with others. Just imagine that!
It is for finding and sharing and celebrating *fully aliveness* that we come to church.

"Read all about it! Hot off the press! Fully aliveness found in local church. Read all about it!"
(Does that thought confound your expectations?)

Simeon and Anna looked at each other in amazement.
It was astonishing how, at moments of prophecy, their minds met in synchronicity.
"Fully aliveness—in West Didsbury?" chuckled Anna. "Who'd have believed it?"
"Who indeed," wondered Simeon. "But where's West Didsbury?"

Fully aliveness in a church? In this church?
A wild, crazy, dream?
Then dare to say yes to it! Imagine it
into becoming! Pray it
into reality! Birth it
into being! Weave it
into your lives!Say yes! Or
is the threat of life to much to bear?
Say yes!

And see
God get down off her dusty pillar,
climb onto the back of her tiger, (yes!),
and come striding down among us. (Nodding in a familiar way to each of us in turn.)

The Lord suddenly—and so very
unexpectedly—coming into the Temple!

Luke 5:1-11

Crithmum maritimum
Rock Samphire

"The plant's common name, from the French 'herbe Saint-Pierre,' refers to St Peter, the 'rock' : patron saint of fishermen."

06 Lakeside Sermon
(Luke 5:1-11)

An important ecumenical church was setting about the serious business of choosing three new pastors. The appointment panel asked the Catholic candidates for the post to say Mass. The best one got the job. The panel asked the Free Church candidates to preach a sermon. The best one got the job. And, then, for the Anglican candidates ... to organize a yard or jumble sale!
The moral of the story, told to me by a Methodist minister, is never to ask Anglicans to preach.

Hmm.

Now, I find myself with the bizarre thought that, had Jesus been one of the candidates at that church, they wouldn't have
dared
ask him to organize a yard or jumble sale—for fear he'd have overturned all the tables. So would they instead have asked him to celebrate the Last Supper? Again? Or would they have asked him to preach, just like he used to do?

Just like he used to do ....

Jesus stepped into one of the boats, the one belonging to Simon, And asked him to put out a little way from the shore. Then he sat down and addressed the crowds.

I wonder whether you are the sort of people who have sermon survival techniques.
Do you have supplies of sweets and candies hidden upon your person?
Do you pass the time reading the smallest details of news on the pew sheet?
Or finding your favorite hymn in the hymnbook?
Or counting the windows, the chairs, the stains on the carpet?
Checking for damp patches in the roof? Staring at the floor? Or guessing how long the preacher will go on for?
(And what are you hoping for today?)

*The crowd strained to hear what Jesus was saying as the wind blew away his words
So he stood up and raised his voice.*

I guess you know that there are two common words for this bit of the service. The one often used in Catholic churches is "homily." The word homily originally meant a lecture or talk explaining the meaning of the Bible texts. But the more familiar word, perhaps, is "sermon," from the French word "sermonner" meaning "to tell off." A chance for the pastor to tell the people off for whatever wayward behavior *you've* been up to during the past week!

In English, the word "sermon" has many negative overtones: to sermonize, to preach, to correct, to exhort, to put people "right." To show you the error of *your* ways!

In the past, the sermon could often be an hour or two in length and take a day or two to write.
And, even now, Anglican canon law states that if there is no minister to preach the word of God then it is the duty of the churchwardens to read from the Book of Homilies, (each sermon twenty-five pages long, but seeming *infinitely* longer!) which, according to a law passed in the reign of the first queen Elizabeth, should be found in every parish church in England.

Sermons have changed their form and meaning over time. When John Wesley
was training his ministers, they were told to "break

open the word of God so that men may apply it to their lives and be nourished." While, when Baptist preachers were being trained, they were told to
"SHOUT LOUDLY!"
if their argument was at any point weak.
(A device still used by some evangelists to this day.)

But all of this begs the question, for the modern preacher, of what one is supposed to do in this curious space called sermon.

Do people come to church expecting to be morally admonished—or just bored?
Should the preacher seek to offer some serious teaching in the five or ten minutes before people starting reaching the outer limits of their attention span?
Is the sermon an opportunity to convince? Or else to
convert?
Should I have visual aids, or ask you to stand up and be involved in some cringe-worthy way?
(Would it be a good idea at this point to break up into small groups and discuss the Bible readings in order to work out a strategy for evangelism?)

We do not know what Jesus said that day beside the Lake of Genessaret;
his words have blown away on the winds of time. But
after he'd finished, and the crowd took his message excitedly home
for supper,
Jesus asked his disciples to row out into deeper water. Now Simon Peter and his men were exhausted after a long night's fishless fishing, but ... "if you say so,
Lord."
And what happened next shocked them to the core and changed their lives
for ever. For
the unthinkable happened.

Now my theory is that the sermon is the place in the normally very familiar service when the unthinkable might just happen.
When the congregation—you—might just be persuaded to step outside the memorized words and actions of the liturgy
and think the unthinkable. To think new thoughts and contemplate the possibility of being
"other
than you are."

But, since the congregation never wants to do this, the preacher has to be cunning-creative and have a touch of the poetic.
in order to get under people's skin, make them itch mentally
and, in scratching their heads and hearts,
open up a chink in the armor of their religious routines.
To use their imaginations which, *they always have trouble realizing,* is that part of their nature which comes closest to God's.
That part of *our nature* which comes closest to God's. Imagine that!

"Imagine that!" thought Simon. (And everyone who saw it.)
Suddenly their nets were full. Bursting
apart. Stretched

to breaking point—just like their minds.
Years of fishermen's yarns pulled into holes
by the biggest, tallest, weirdest fisherman's story of them all ...
Familiar reliable reality overturned by the utterly unexpected.
Words failed them, but they were hooked!

Preaching—like hooking people with a good yarn—is all about opening up "a space for poetry in a world flattened by prose."[6]
A time-aside from daily speech, where nothing is normal because everything is possible;
a risky place, precarious;
a place for the unexpected;
a liminal place; a doorway
into another world where
words and meanings tumble around each other and refuse to make just one sense.
A place for pondering,
a place for catching just a
movement
beneath the waves, a
glimpse
of a fish, a flash
of the hand of the divine
as it moves among us, bestirring us, surprising us, recreating us.

A place for hearing echoes of a strangely familiar voice recalling us to some
half-forgotten-remembered purpose,
urging us to explore our deepest desires and to speak out and to share whatever little we know, whatever little faith *we think we* have.

A place for nurturing,
for testing out those unbelievable fishermen's tales and tasting those extravagant kingdom recipes
passed down to us in the stories of the God who in Jesus fed thousands.

A place for believing
and for allowing the spark of the divine to rekindle in us
a flame and a passion and a longing
to proclaim the stern justice and ever gratuitous love of God in a needy world.

A space for answering yes, again
and again and again
in the silence of our hearts and
for realizing that, despite the worst we can offer, God really is there for us.
Always and forever, and forever, and forever.

While the others struggled with the unexpected bonus of a mighty catch,
mentally counting already the extra coins at the fish market,
Simon Peter knelt down ... and was afraid.
A space had opened up in the fabric of his world and, through it, he saw into another place.
Into another reality, more clear, more real than anything he'd known before.

[6] Walter Brueggemann, *Finally Comes the Poet: Daring Speech for Proclamation,* Minneapolis: Fortress Press, 1989, *passim.*

A place where prosaic prose is banished and truth is brought to speech in strange new words:
singing us into life,
rhyming us into being,
coupling us with new ways of living,
reeling us in, hooked, with *baited* breath,
and versing us in the experience of novelty, newness, aliveness, incarnation, resurrection.
Teaching us how to know, and how to utter
Easter.

This
is the task to which each of us is called. For
just as fishermen must tell tales
(of those that got away,
tales of fishy struggles and "herring-do")
just so we Christians, named from Christ himself,
must speak of the God "who gives life to the dead, and who calls into being things that do not exist"
(Romans 4:17).

Jesus raised Simon to his feet. "Don't be afraid," he said. "From now on ..."

Don't be afraid, for from now on
we
can all discover
what happened next.
For what happened next ... can happen *now*.

We just need to hear the call
and answer yes again
and again and again in the silence of our hearts
And realize that, despite the worst we can and do offer, God really is
there for us.
Always and forever, and forever, and forever, and ...

Matthew 4:1-11

WIN
TER

Atropa belladonna
Deadly Nightshade

"Every part of the Atropa belladonna is toxic and attacks the central nervous system making the heart race and the pulse weaken. Local names include "Devil's berries," "Satan's cherries," and "Devil's rhubarb."

07 Deadly Nightshade
(Matthew 4:1-11)

(Just look at him, sitting there under the burning sun, with just a snake to watch over him.
How long's he been there now? It must be days and days.
We thinks he must be hungry by now. We thinks he must be famished, poor thing. Famished.
Let's see if we can offer him something tempting.)

Look at all these big hard stones: round, just like fine large loaves.
Stones: round, just like bread, my precious.
Go on—you can do it. Go on; it's not difficult.
Don't doubt yourself!

Oh yes; we knows what you're thinking. We can get inside your head. We can feel your hunger, we can.

It's alright to doubt. We understands, we does.
But you can do it. Just think it; just will it; just imagine it; and then just
taste that soft bread
and lovely crust. Melts
in your mouth it does. Yes.
We knows you'd like that. Make it happen.
After all you've gone through
you deserve it; you're worth it!

Yes—we knows what the scriptures says. We knows every word. Every little word of it—by heart, we does. By heart. By heart. By heart.
But
does it really apply to *you*? For you knows whose son you are. Doesn't you? Doesn't you?
And won't ... HE ... make an exception for you? You of all people ...

(Just look at him now, sitting there in the cold darkness, holding a scorpion in his little hands. His only friend!
Oh we feels his pain we does. We knows the sting of all the suffering he's going through.
We pities him, we does. Doesn't we? Yes! Poor thing. All alone in the dark.
Let's us brighten him up. Bring him some comfort.)

All alone, my little one? Yes we knows!
If you was our son we wouldn't abandon you like this, would we? No, not us.
We'd be good to you, we would.
We'd spend time with you; we'd look after you;
We'd love you and have fun with you.
We wouldn't ignore you like this.

Come with us now.
We knows a nice place. High up. A tall tower.
If we takes you there and you jumps off ... HE ... HE'll come running and catch you up.
Come back to you and comfort you.
And if not, well, we'll save you and love you instead. Yes we will!
You can trust us you can.
We'd never let you down. No!
You can count on us, you can; my little one. Count on us.
No it's not a test my precious one. No—we was just

concerned for you.
Just wants you to be alright, we does.
We is your friend, we is.
Watching over you, like a real father, my little one. Watching ...

(Just look at him now. Muttering to himself. Walking in circles. Right up to the mountain top.
It's been so very long. And he's so very weak. Lost all his strength, he has, poor thing.
All his strength is gone.
He needs building up! Needs his strength and power back!)

Don't get too close to the edge, little one. Step back. Don't fall!

Oh! But look at the view. Oh we loves the view we does.
Often comes up here to watch.
The world is so very big; and so many people to watch over!
You could help us, you could.
A man like you would make a fine ruler. The very best!
We'd give it all to you, we would.
Trust it all to you. Oh yes we would. Everything! Everything!
All we'd ask is just for us to be your friend. Your real friend. Your best friend. Your only friend. No one else. Just us.
Oh how we'd like that!

Then Jesus spoke.
"Worship the Lord your God and serve only him."

Just look at them now. All sitting quietly—in rapt attention. Listening.
They all knows this story. Off by heart they does. Off by heart.
Don't even have to think about it anymore does they? No.
A story all about us. Our story. We likes that. Nice!!

Every year they reads it.
And every year they thinks they understands it.
(Just like we wants them to.)

They tries to resist just like ... HE ... did.
And we likes to watch them. Oh yes we does! Just like we've always done.
We watches.

They gives up their chocolate, they does.
Chocolate and booze!
"Lenten detox" they calls it. It's trendy now. All doing it, they is.
Just like we wants them to.
Just like we wants them to.

And while they is counting their calories and feeling grand and holy
We carries on with our real work.
And they never notices! No.
They never notices!

They believes how all that matters is giving up what they likes.
Chocolate and booze and nice things. "Extras." They just gives up their "extras"!
While we ... finds ways of keeping others hungry.
While we ... winds the world up in red tape and politics.
While we ... keeps stirring up hatred and confusion.
While we ... reeks havoc and unrest.
While we ... stops good things, creative things, HIS things, from happening.
And they never notices!

We tempts them to think trivial things is all that matters.
And they never sees it; never catches on!

They thinks we's tempting them *real hard*, the poor things.
But they misses the point, they does.
They can't think outside their chocolate box!

So each year we gets the upper hand just a *little bit*
more.
And they goes on ignoring the things that really matters.
Not troubling to get involved in things that could really make a difference.
Ignoring what we're really up to!

That's the truth of it. That's the truth!!
Cos we never lies, does we? We never lies. Oh no!
And you believes us. Don't you? So,

will you let us be your friend ...?

Sermons 08 - 12
SPR
ING

Matthew 19:27-30; Acts 9:1-22

Spring leaves

08 Could I Ask You a Question?

(Matthew 19:27-30; Acts 9:1-22)

Well, thank you for coming. We just have one more question for you.
Could you tell us, please, how, where, and when you were converted?

Now there's a question I wasn't expecting—at *any* interview—not even at this one for a Christian charity.
I took a moment—such an eternity it seemed— before replying.
But what could I say?

Flash back to St Paul. And flash indeed!
A blinding flash of inspiration under the noonday sun.
A man of radical convictions stopped dead in his tracks. Felled
like a mighty tree, sent
crashing to the ground, turned
bodily upside down, and shaken
till the loose change of his former life falls out and rolls away.
Gone forever. In a flash:
converted

from one set of certainties,
from safe, well-brought-up assumptions and practiced routines
from one life-long common sense,
from one well-tried way of ordering life and worshiping of God:
converted
to the possibility—the possibility—of an other. Led away

into a nearby town,
to hospitality amongst strangers and a quiet room in the house of Judas.

Here Saul-Paul has space to ponder the unexpected hyphen between his two identities;
space to ponder and to explore the confusion of his mind
and its freshly-violated limits.
Time to consent to the possibility in his soul
that the life-giving words of Torah had been forever re-arranged:
translated into a different language,
by a living word speaking to his heart,
calling him by name.

I squirmed in the chair. They smiled patiently.
What answer would suit them?
Did they want fireworks? All I had was a smoldering fire.
Did they want razzamatazz? All I had was the little tune I often hum to myself.
Did they want to hear my certain convictions? All I had were questions, doubts, and suspicions.
Oh, that I had been converted like they wanted!
Still they smiled. The sort of smile that anticipates victory. Ha! Caught him out!

Saul-Paul sat and pondered, entombed in his darkness, until
bit by bit,
moment by moment, hour by hour,
a slow eternity of three long days passed
and the light returned.

SPR
ING

*He tried to explain it all to Ananias and to the other disciples
who ventured in to peer suspiciously at this most unexpected of houseguests.
How had it happened? What exactly did it mean?*

Now converted was I never. If,
for conversion,
Paul is the norm.
But if, for conversion, we read a slow-fast, fits-and-starts, growing,
movement by degrees:
conversion by a myriad moments of grace,
an erratic stream of quite ordinary insights,
a smile or tone of voice,
a gesture of welcome,
an autumn leaf falling, just so,
a bar of music,
a gospel story,
a righting of wrongs and kingdom-justice done,
each insight adding its feather-light weight to
tip my mind towards assenting to a curious possibility in my soul …

If this counts for conversion,
then conversion is indeed the road I'm traveling!

*Traveling
was Paul's life. (Before and after.)
And still it was destined so to be; though now to a different end and destination.
Traveling.
He was on the road, you see—Damascus-bound—when it had happened. On the road.
On the way.
And so it had to be:
for conversion only happens when you're somewhere-bound.*

He said that bit again. Slowly. Ananias and the others listened carefully:
"Conversion only happens when you're on the way somewhere."
They all sat in silence thinking hard about that.
"You have to be on the move, he said,
going places,
if you want to be surprised on the way by the living God.
Be met on the road and have your life transformed."

Life transformed.

As for Paul, so for me.
I discovered that conversion—however it happens—only happens
when we're on the move.
Forwards. Outwards. Upwards. Onwards.
(What about you?)

When we
dare ourselves to go beyond where we are,
stepping outside of the boxes we inhabit.
(What about you?)

When we
urge ourselves to go further than we'd really like, or planned;
going beyond our comfort zone, overstepping the mark, into unsafe territory.
(Eyes watching, fingers pointing, tongues wagging
at us.)

When we
brave ourselves over and across the secure frontiers of our known world,
"boldly going where we have not gone before."
(What about you?)

When we
let the Spirit open us up
and draw us on,
though a continuous process of seeking and finding
encountering and learning,
calling and responding,
daring and risking,
falling and rising, again and again,
inviting, welcoming, befriending, and challenging.
(What about you?)

All this Paul tried to explain. ("And what about you?" he asked them.)
The disciples frowned. In disbelief, possibly.

And all this I tried to explain.

But their smiles faded as they listened.
(And what about you?)

So we—Paul and I—tried explaining again. Following a different track this time.

Conversion isn't
to a secure place beyond doubt or danger.
Conversion isn't
a once-and-for-all leaping onto a safe plateau, thankfully high above the raging waves of inner turmoil. (No waves lapping at your feet.)
Conversion is
a risk-filled process of becoming;
a process of exposing ourselves willingly to all that lies beyond our present horizon
to what is beckoning us
(can you see it?),
to what is summoning us, calling us

(can you hear it, just?),
to what is *urging us, daring us to follow*
(can you feel it, tugging?)

Daring us to be like Jesus.
(To be like Jesus—Paul's voice trembled here)
by consenting to walk the road of possibility;
and by staking high on that possibility
that, in risking
everything, all and more will be found.

And then by coming to the end of what you know,
and feel,
from a source beyond it, a certain something
filling your being with its possibilities
urging you out and up and over. Ever further on, further on, further on ...

Come. Let's walk with Paul.
Let's step out from this place into the daylight.
Let's take a risk. Risk everything: for what have we got to lose?

Think, instead, of the possibilities.
Think of all that will come from reaching out,
out towards all those who peer suspiciously inside, not daring to come in,
to all those who frown in disbelief
to all those who want to understand
to all those who want to find the way to start ...

Well, thank you for coming. I just have one more question for you.
Could you tell me, please ...?

Flash back again to St Paul.
Immediately he began to proclaim Jesus,
and all who heard him were amazed and said:
When and where were you converted? Tell us!

For which of us can avoid what we must become?
What do *you* say?

So. Can I ask you a question?

Exodus 17:1-7
John 4:5-42

SPR
ING

Aloe Vera

Spiky desert aloes

09 A Spot of Bother
(Exodus 17:1-7; John 4:5-42)

To say they were in a spot of bother was an understatement. All around them,
prickling their bodies, like the spikes of the rough desert plants strewn along their path,
burning their skin,
and drying up their bones, was
the merciless desert sun, beating everything to the ground.
All around them the people cried for water.
And when the sun went down and the chill of the desert night settled upon the huddled crowd
up went another
more chilling cry still,
sending waves of panic and terror into the hearts of Moses and Joshua and those hand-picked elders.
"Is the L ORD among us—or not?"
"Is the L ORD *among us*—or not?"
"Is the L ORD among us—*or not*?"
"Should we blame Moses, or should we blame God?"
"Oh that we had stayed where we were in Egypt! At least we had water."
"Water, water ... We are thirsty ... So thirsty ..."

To say they were in a spot of bother was an understatement.
Moses had tried to lead them, tried to follow God's
promptings, God's clues, God's signs, God's

urgings. But it was never easy.
For God had such a way of
always
doing the unexpected, the miraculous; such a way
of stretching people's minds and souls in directions they never expected.
Moses never ceased to be surprised and amazed.
And often not a little apprehensive!
(You know the feeling, no doubt.)

But in this desert, this wasteland seemingly so empty of hope,
Moses was close to giving up. Close
to handing back his staff of office and swapping it for the shepherds' crook of his younger days. For
"All they do is quarrel, and moan; whatever I try never
satisfies them. I can never
satisfy their needs. I'm wasting
my life in this wasteland," he whispered.
"But Lord ...You *are* still with us? Aren't you?"

The idea of striking
the rock, didn't strike
Moses as all that odd.
He knew what God
could do when God drew that bright mantle of glory around herself.
And the rest of the story is, as they say, "herstory." Then
out gushed the water!
They were so *thirsty* and it tasted like ...well,
like water from heaven itself!
(Had bottles been around, they'd have bottled it!

09 A Spot of Bother

As it was, they settled for a skinful.) My, it was good!
That night, as the people slept, they dreamed of the deep wellsprings they'd seen back in Egypt.
And, their thirst satisfied at last, they heard
from deep in their dreams,
the sound of a half-forgotten-remembered voice
calling them. Each
by their own name ...

The noonday sun struck out relentlessly, beating everything to the ground. Jesus lay, propped up against a date palm which grew at the side of the well.
In the heat he thought he heard a voice, half-forgotten-remembered,
calling him.

He awoke and heard a woman singing to herself. He was so *thirsty*!
All around him, prickling his body,
like the spikes of the rough desert plants strewn along the path,
burning into his skin and drying up his bones,
was the merciless desert sun. All around him
his body cried for water.
"Woman," he called. "Bring me some water ... I thirst."

She watched him drink. Amazed
not only because of how much he drank,
but of the matter-of-fact way he asked her. Had the heat driven him crazy?

For what usually passed between Jews and Samaritans were looks of scorn; each for the other.
Centuries
of mistrust, centuries
of stand-offs, centuries
of hurtful stories, slander, and bitterness.
And who was he—in this noonday heat—to cast aside all these centuries?

(And a man, too, she thought. And she a woman.
And why did he address her so ... intimately; this guy?
Oh yes; she knew all about intimacy, all about flirting, nodding, and winking.
No innuendo was ever lost on her. She was an old hand at those games! But this guy
wasn't after playing that oldest of games. This guy
wasn't up for any *heated* encounter under the noonday sun, even with the ample opportunity of this totally deserted spot.)

Yet, despite his own need—this guy—
he saw her greater thirst.
She offered him water and watched while he drank, this guy;
but he returned a gaze that entered her soul, this guy:
drawing to its surface more than any bucket could hold.

To say she was in a spot of bother was an understatement.
(You know the feeling, no doubt.)

SPR
ING

But the idea of striking at the heart of her need didn't strike Jesus as all that odd.
He knew what God could do when God drew that bright mantle of glory around herself.
And the rest, as they say, is "herstory." Well: her story
and our story …

To say we are in a spot of bother is an understatement.
All around us, prickling our bodies, like the spikes of the rough desert plants strewn along our path,
burning into our skin and drying up our bones,
is the merciless sun, in a desert of indifference.
No-one seems to come any more.
No want wants to visit these ancient wells of ours.
Yet all the while
our own people shout and argue, blame and curse each other—while
those around us cry out
for spiritual drink.

And when the sun goes down and the chill of the night settles upon the huddled crowds, blank-faced
before their TV screens,
up goes another
more chilling cry still,
sending waves of panic and terror into the hearts of our leaders and our hand-picked elders.
"Is there hope among us—or not?"
"Is there a vision anywhere among us—or not?"
"Is the Lord here with us—*or not*?" God

prompted Moses to strike at the rock, and out came living water. God
urged Moses to take his staff, the symbol of God's
authority, and use it to bring life, from what was dead:
new life from the accumulated layers of dust from their ancient past.
And from the lifeless rock of that barren
wasteland, came flowing water for the thirsty:
new strength, new hope, a new vision, a new passion for the journey that lay ahead. God

urged Jesus to strike out at what was dead,
at those accumulated layers of dust from the past,
at those weighty layers of vacuous authority,
at those structures and divisions preserved-to-the-death by those with vested interests
at those petrified attitudes and habits that might once have brought life, long ago.

And from somewhere deep within him, Jesus draws up a force of living water;
water to sweep away those old orders of custom, prejudice, assumption, and long-meaningless tradition
water to tear up the rubble blocking the head of the living well
So that all might drink again.

As a church we are poised today on the knife
edge of something extraordinary. We are
in crisis.
Just around the corner: extinction, perhaps; yet just over there life,
can be imagined. Perhaps.

And all around us the people are thirsty; crying out for life.
Yet—largely through our own myopic wandering and rambling—we find ourselves in a desert place,
surrounded by the needles of our sharp dilemmas,
(all at sea, and no water!)
and no way out. Apparently.
So stay here—increasingly uncomfortable—in our last years, and then die, unmourned;
or else move forward into the future? And risk finding fresh water and a new vision.

Shall we opt to shore up our crumbling structures until,
with our last breathe gone we fall, crushed and buried, under their weight?
Shall we opt to stay hiding where we are,
polishing, over and over, the now wafer-thin glories of yesteryear? Or

do we instead dare to strike out for the future,
opening ourselves up to the God who can bring living water from dead rock
opening ourselves up to the God who earnestly calls us, each one of us, each one of us,
to move on from where we are,
and to set aside our pre-occupations with things that distract us from what really matters
to become instead a community where all can find their thirst satisfied?

Brothers and sisters,
fellow Christians of long-standing and good faith,
leaders and elders of your communities:
to say we're in a spot of bother is an understatement.

We are in the desert, the sun is beating down and
all around the people are crying and dying of thirst. So what
are we going to do?

1 Kings 18; 2 Kings 4; John 2: 1-11

Vines

10 Drinking Deep

(1 Kings 18; 2 Kings 4; John 2:1-11)

This being a sermon in part at least about wine,
I took myself off to a wine bar with pen and paper to wait for inspiration.
But would the spirit come? And what would that spirit have me speak?

A friend of mine—a great lover of wine—helpfully calculated
that the six stone water jars of the biblical proportions we heard described this morning
tot nicely up to 1200 bottles of top shelf vintage. Quite a wedding gift!

My friend then surmised that
if-an-average-guest-drank-one-bottle-then-it-was-quite-some-wedding-celebration-too!
And miraculous
to the extent that is was saved from disaster by
(how did he do it?
a wink of an eye, perhaps?
or by a discreet wave of the hand?)
the first of the signs that Jesus made.

A sign of something bigger than himself.
The sign of a God for whom there are no half measures, no
stinting; and nothing
grudgingly given.
The mark of a God of extravagant gestures, boundless acts of love, and overwhelming hospitality.
(Cheers! L'chayyim!)
The attribute of a God who knows how to celebrate. How
to throw a party.
A party with enough—and more!—for everyone.
A party where everyone is welcome.
A party to break the mould for parties.

(Now that's quite some first sign, isn't it?
Quite some way for Jesus to begin his ministry.
A tough act to follow you might say.
And yet he was to manage even that.)

Of course, we know with our heads that if
God is God then God
can—and will—do anything:
(with the wink of an eye, perhaps,
or by a discreet wave of the hand).
It has ever been thus
it is ever thus—when the living God is at work.

But, if we're honest, it makes us feel uncomfortable,
this winking of an eye and discreet waving of a hand.
And so we find ourselves wanting to put limits on God's generosity,
on God's gratuitous-riotous-delicious love
for God's creation and for all the people,
all the people,
all the people without exception
that God has made.

We look about us at the party and say—why are *they* here?
Surely not *them*?
Why is God talking with them, when *we're* over here?
Why is God laughing and joking with their sort?
Why is God wasting the best wine on them?
Why not give us some more—and offer them
something (*just a bit*)
less expensive, something for *less*
discerning palates. They won't notice. And they'll be so grateful!

And then we think: "surely,
Lord, this is just all too much! (We're only thinking about you. The trouble and the expense!)
Draw the line somewhere.
Don't use up *everything* you've got.
Save it for later; when we
come back again.
For we will.
They are not worthy to gather up the crumbs under your table.
Not like us."

But God just goes on pouring, pouring, pouring.
And it never runs out... Here. Have this one on him...

Consider, please, Elijah the Tishbite of Tisbe.
There was a drought in the land. (No water, never mind wine!)
But, despite this, Elijah took himself off to the driest place in that driest drought. Down

by the wadi of Cherith he acted out his trust
that God
(the generous, the loving, the beneficent)
would provide.
And so the ravens fed him. Bread and meat twice a day. (Room service with wings!)

And then (to make the point still further, there being too few people around the wadi to get the message)
that Tishbite of Tisbe found himself a widow woman in the town,
collecting sticks she was, to make a last supper
for herself and her son.
A meal to use up what was left—and then to die;
a handful of flour at the bottom of her pot and some dregs of oil in her jug.

But that remnant didn't give out.
It didn't give out.
It didn't give out.
It didn't give out.
It never ran dry—she just went on pouring, pouring, pouring.
She trusted God's generosity. And
it never gave out.
It never gave up ...

10 Drinking Deep

Here's a secret. (Do you like secrets?) Listen.
When reading the stories of Elijah the Tishbite of Tisbe (in 1 Kings)
always turn over a few pages (to 2 Kings)
to see what Elijah's *alter ego* Elisha is getting up to.
For often what Elijah likes, Elisha likes to go one better.

Now Elisha's also at a wadi. The driest place in the drought.
In this story God floods that dry place with water—as far as the eye can see.
(Just to show them!)
And God has Elisha go into town find a widow woman of his own.
A woman with creditors hammering at her door and nothing
whatsoever
to pay them with:
just a few dregs of oil at the bottom of her jug.
"Pour it." says Elisha. "Pour it and keep on pouring, pouring, pouring.
Send your sons and daughters to borrow pots and pans: and fill them up too.
All the way! Draw deep from God's boundless generosity!
And don't stop till everyone's pot is full!"
For God is a generous giver. More than we can ever imagine, imagine, imagine ...

Imagine. For 2000 years and more, we've had time to imagine.
Time and enough for opportunities to act! To do like God does.
But what have we made of this generous time and enough?
What have we done with this vision of plenty-and-enough-for-all?
What have we done in the name of the God who invites all and everyone to the party?

We've built walls around the house and put rules upon the door.
We've drawn up guest lists of our own devising and paid minders to maintain our order.
We've pulled down that edifice of generosity and set up a pale, lifeless, imitation.
A mean place, full of scowls and fists clenched tight, throttling God's words of life. And

worst of all we've convinced not only ourselves of our own holiness,
but those we exclude of *their own unworthiness*. And
(with the wink of an eye, perhaps,
or by a discreet wave of the hand)
we
ostracise, we
deny, we
curse, and we
damn. We
extol the narrow-minded, the mealy-mouthed, the stone-hearted and the anally retentive.
And then we
wonder why no-one comes any more.
And why the party's almost over;
done to death by drought and famine.
(Our souls shrivelled. Spiritless.)

Have we forgotten *everything*?

SPR
ING

Have we *anything* left to offer?

Can we
open our souls up—wide and big enough—
to trust the boundlessness of God's love?
To feel again the hot passion of God's loving? Can we
recognize our folly and repent? Can we? Can we
ever learn to imagine and so embody God again? Can we? Can we
still dare take in our hands the cup of life and drink deep, a draught to heal our souls?
and offer it to bring life to others, can we?
And be for others an open invitation to the party, can we?
Transforming the world around us with a "welcome," can we?
Making even the driest places of our world—and the church—
(with the wink of an eye, perhaps,
or by a discreet wave of the hand)
a place where the spirit just goes on pouring, pouring, pouring...
can we?

We have to
believe we can.

And the challenge begins right now.
It's your round.

John 13:31-35

SPR
ING

Adoxa moschatellina
Moschatel

Lilium
Lillies

"The word 'Adoxa' comes from the Greek meaning 'without glory,' from its apparent small and insignificant status.
There are about 110 species in the lily family, all with pollen-laden stamens."

11 The Dust of Glory
(John 13:31-35) [7]

I find very odd. This business about glory.
And I'm uneasy and confused. So
I took a big book down from the library shelf and had a root around. It said:
"glory is the fundamental characteristic of God to which believers respond by giving glory to God" (In other words, God has glory and so, in response, we give God more glory?)

Then it said:
"glory in people takes the form of wealth, position and power" (anyone here fit that bill?) and "people give more glory to God when we sing and pray or are still before God."

And finally it said:
"all *serious* Christian thinkers acknowledge that giving glory to God is what human life is really about."

(Hmm!)

I've thought long about this all week and I've been trying hard to be aware,
as the week has progressed,
of how we people—and also I in my life—have been giving glory to God. Or not.

Was it the students' Christian Union who on Thursday came to the end of a mammoth ten-day-non-stop-prayer-session-for-the-conversion-of-the-world?
(A spiritual decathlon if ever there was.)
Did that glorify God? Or
was it the university chaplaincy when we welcomed the Buddhist society to come and make a home with us and begin the process of making the chaplaincy multi-faith?
Did that offer God glory? Or
was it the many lectures and seminars and classes this past week on every aspect of human life and existence? Or
the many hours of therapeutic activities on campus—sport, counseling, free legal aid, the new staff mentoring scheme? Or,
wider afield, was it the war in Iraq and those alleged photos of abuse?
Was it the UN Security Council's decision not to intervene in the crisis in Sudan? Or else perhaps Marseille's soccer victory over Newcastle United?

More specifically:
can we and do we
give glory to God by every small act of kindness;
or is glory only there when one pours out one's life?

All I know and feel at the end of this week's events and revelations is that I'm not sure any more. Despite the post-Easter optimism I generally bask in, this week I'm left feeling
adrift;
circling round my own humanity in a sea of doubts. Wondering
about my own nature and that of my fellow humans.

Now don't get me wrong.
Generally I'm an over-optimistic sort with boundless belief in humanity.
For years I've preached that, in the words of Saint Irenaeus, "the glory of God is a person who is fully alive."

---

[7] Preached after the publication of pictures of the abuse of Iraqi prisoners.

And I've tried to celebrate, promote, and embody that aliveness where ever I've been.
(I'm really no good at any other sort of ministry.)

But this week I've been taking refuge in our two cats who
seem to make a better job of aliveness and of glorifying God than we do.
They have been my solace. My soul friends.
For, all week long, they've been going about *just being cats*.
With no pretensions to being anything else.

Perhaps, I thought, nothing we can ever do can make a difference.
Perhaps that's what Jesus' words mean: "where I am going, you cannot come."
Perhaps there is, after all, an unbridgeable gulf between us and God
and God is unaffected by anything we do.
Perhaps our glory, thrown up like pebbles at the Almighty's window, merely
bounces off and falls to earth. Unable
to disturb the Lord's intent.
(There is, after all a strand of Christian thinking which says as much.
Perhaps I am becoming a Barthian?)

But then, yesterday, Cyril came to my rescue. Not another saint, but a window cleaner.
Or a saint in a window cleaner's chamois.
Cyril just goes about being a window cleaner. Our window cleaner.
Except that yesterday he also helped to clean my spiritual vision. The windows of my soul.

For, from his bucket, he took out love
(an unorthodox tool for cleaning windows. Heretical.)
He took out love, as needful for human flourishing as water is for human life.
(Or windows.)
He took out love.
He told me of his love of the church. (In his boy scouting days, at least! Now he prefers to admire the windows from outside. Professionally.)
He told me of his love of the community, his friendships, his awareness of the transience of our lives, and then he smiled.
And went on his way, cleaning windows. Unaware of the shaft of light he'd blessed me with.

But is there still love left in our buckets at the end of this week?

Judas had just left to go about his deeds of darkness.
And now Jesus got up to depart for a different destiny.
A once-for-all destiny;
a believe-it-if-you-dare sort of destiny;
the sort destiny that can bridge all kinds of gaps and clean all kinds of souls.

As he turned to go he looked over his shoulder. "Where I am going, you cannot come," he said. And seeing their confusion
he paused.
"But here's a new commandment. Something to ponder
when I'm not here, and to help you on your way.
(One of you, write it down.)

You've seen how I've loved you. And there's more to come.
But now you—love one another. Like I showed you.
Well—try to. And keep trying.
Try with ever fiber of your being. And never give up.

When things look bleak, at the end of an awful week
Pick yourselves up and dust yourselves down.
Take each other by the hand and start off again.
Remind each other that you are precious in God's eyes
and that each one of you
(he pointed silently around the room)
is of infinite value. But
don't get sentimental about this."

For loving one another—especially those we don't like or can't understand, or
those whose language and religion is different, or
whose habits seem strange, whose lifestyle isn't ours or
whose suffering and exploitation have made them bitter—
loving one another is
a tough hard business.
A job for realists.

For the green and grassy path of loving
soon gives way to the rough terrain of justice making
and to bearing the heavy load of responsibility for what goes on in this world,
whose making we share with God.

If we want to follow Jesus out of that room,
(or want to want to),
if we want to play a part
in shaping what lies around us,
then we need to develop the art,
experiment with the recipe,
that Jesus showed us, gave us, left us. Taking

the human love we all share, and mixing
it with courage and determination and
a large dose of imagination to see the world through others' eyes. And then
applying it,
liberally, generously, gratuitously
to whatever it is we do,
to where ever it is we are,
to how ever it is we live.

And then to discover at the end of an awful week
the dust of God's glory on our hands.

Acts 8:26-40; John 15:1-8

SPRING

Heather

12 The Great Queen's Treasurer

(Acts 8:26-40; John 15:1-8)

He was thrown side-ways and dust flew up into his face. He began to choke. Barking some obscenity at his driver, he found his place again on the scroll. Again he read it. But what did it mean? How could it help make sense of things?

Today's sermon is not for the squeamish.
It's about eunuchs; eunuchs becoming fruitful.
Yes. A logical impossibility, perhaps! But listen on …

Now, we may not know many eunuchs these days,
But perhaps we all know something of what it feels like to be impotent; impotent
to do anything,
to change anything: about us, or about the world.
And perhaps we also know a thing or two about wanting to be fruitful.
Perhaps we've always wanted—deep down—to be really happy, successful, fulfilled;
to be fruitful and flourishing?

And many people—like our eunuch friend—
still dip into the scriptures to find a clue, a hint; some guidance for what to do next. Answers to our burning
questions.
And often we are attracted to passages that seem to resonate with our own condition.
It's not a new phenomenon. (Perhaps you've done the same. I have.)

Now we don't know his name—even though we are witnesses at his baptism—but
our eunuch friend was doing just that too. Finding a passage of scripture
that would somehow speak to his experience.

Bumping along the desert road, he tried to follow the scroll with his finger, until he found this:
"Like a sheep he was lead to the slaughter …
like a lamb silent before its shearer …"

The thought of the knife came back to him. He shuddered, but he read on:
"In his humiliation justice was denied him.
Who can describe his generation?
For his life is taken away from the earth."

Of course we know now that he probably read these words in another version.
Not the version we read in Acts, but in Hebrew, as he searched for answers to his questions.
So let's scroll back and start again:

"…like a lamb that is lead to the slaughter …
like a sheep that before its shearers is silent …
By a perversion of justice he was taken away.
  Who could have imagined his future?
For he was cut off from the land of the living … [Isaiah 53:7, 8]."

12 The Great Queen's Treasurer

Perhaps he remembered how, as a small boy, he'd been "taken away by a perversion of justice" from his family
(by soldiers of the royal household).
And then who "*could have imagined his future*"?
For he had been "*cut off from the land of the living:*"
He had been made to enter the Great Queen's service
and, like all so privileged, he had been *cut off* ...
so as to better serve her without
distractions.

But was it worth it?
Did his high status now make up for what he had lost by the knife?
Did his fine robes and fine food and slaves?
Did his power and influence—in charge of the whole treasury?
No. He felt as though his life had been taken away, stolen, wasted. So ...

in his quest for meaning and purpose
(and because self-help groups had not been invented), he
took to religion. He
started attending synagogue and he
was now on the way back from his very first pilgrimage to the Temple itself. Such a building! Although ...
even his diplomatic status had not been enough to get him beyond its outer court.
His black skin had identified him as a foreigner.
And his voice had betrayed his secret
imperfection.
He was taboo!

Of course, writing all this down in his Book of Acts, Luke, tells us that, in his search for meaning and purpose, this unfortunate man was drawn to the passage from Isaiah because it would lead him to Philip and to baptism and to Jesus.
(I know you know I know that,
but I thought it needed mentioning anyway.) So—scroll back yet again, please. Rewind.

If the Great Queen's Treasurer,
thrown by the potholes on the dusty road,
and choking
and shouting obscenities at his driver
and trying to read the prophet Isaiah to find the answers to his life's questions
(Are you still with me? It's quite a ride, isn't it?); if
his hand had moved just an inch or two further down the scroll that fateful day,
he would have read this amazing passage where God says:

"*To the eunuchs who keep my Sabbaths, who choose the things that please me and hold fast to my covenant, I will give, within my house and within my walls, a monument and a name better than sons and daughters; I will give them an everlasting name that shall not be cut off (Isaiah 56: 4,5).*"
Now I'm asking you to make a small leap of the imagination. Just to see where we land.
(Are you okay with that? Here goes.)
Because
it's not beyond the bounds of possibility that

this is actually the place where he'd *started to read* that day. Bouncing
around on that dusty road. Thrown

out of the Temple for being
who-and-what-he-was,
(imagine his rejection, hurt and anger, desperation),
he'd searched the scriptures for that word "eunuch,"
that name "eunuch,"
that people spat at him when he passed by. And look where his search had led him!
It had led him to a promise, from the very lips
of God. A promise:
that faithfulness to God's covenant, faithfulness to being a disciple of God would
bring a blessing better
even than the blessing of having sons and daughters. How his heart must have

leapt
within him! That it was possible for him,
for him, even for him,
to please God and find fulfillment.
To the amazing discovery that—in the kingdom of God—even eunuchs can flourish.
Even eunuchs.

Now these thoughts need not be surprising.
For we know, I think, that Christians believe that the kingdom of God is precisely all about flourishing.
We know too that "church"
albeit it the palest reflection, nothing
more than a weather beaten sign pointing to the way
is *nevertheless* (God help us!) also meant to be a place where people—even eunuchs—
find flourishing and fullness of life.

And we are called
to be fruitful and to flourish. But is that what you feel? Do you
feel the church has helped you feel fulfilled?
Has this church helped you find peace and flourishing?
And do you come to church Sunday by Sunday
excited, anticipating
all the ways in which you will find what you're looking for? And
do you come to church knowing that, as a practicing Christian, it's your responsibility to
help others find what they're looking for? And
do we come to church—clergy and lay folk—concerned to
discover how we ourselves might be the *very thing* that prevents
others from growing in faith and finding fullness of life?
We have a clue.

Jesus' picture of the vine helps us to see that,
if we are to be fruitful,
if we are to find our true purpose,
if we are to find what we've been created for,
if we are to discover what our true destiny is,

12 The Great Queen's Treasurer

if we are to discover our real selves,
if we are to be transformed by the creative power of the Spirit of God,
if we are to change the world, then
we have to do so together.

All of us—together.
Held together by the common belief
that what we are here for,
what we are church for
in this place
is to help each other become more fruitful, more flourishing, more fully human.
Even eunuchs. Especially eunuchs.

And if we can't do this—or find our flourishing—in this place
(and so become a sign of hope for others)
then the church as a whole has no chance of offering healing, wholeness, or flourishing
to the world and its people.
Think on it.

The two men stepped down from the chariot and into the stream of water.
(The government driver watched in amazement as the Grand Treasurer stripped and knelt before the stranger.)
The water fell cool on this hottest of days.
It ran over his body and soaked away into his parched soul.
He didn't need to glance down to see that he was still what he was,
but he felt - oddly - now he was something new.
That he was something different, something else, something more.
That his future had been forever changed.

(Have you ever felt that? Or wanted that?)

Back on his chariot he took up the scriptures again, still looking for clues.
But now there was a purpose, a direction to his reading,
and a whole
life lying ahead of him to be lived out fully, fruitfully; to be a blessing for others.

On he traveled, bumping along the desert road;
dust flying into his face, choking; still—sadly—barking the occasional obscenity at his driver.
He was on the start of a challenging journey and had much to learn as he went.
And perhaps he is traveling still...

But he had learned that he was not traveling alone,
that there are many of us who feel as he did, many of us who still long for change, fulfillment,
and wholeness.
Our journey begins again today.
His story is his gift to us.
Take heart and follow. Are you ready?
For your story begins again,
right now.
Just make a leap of your imagination and ...

John 5: 1-9

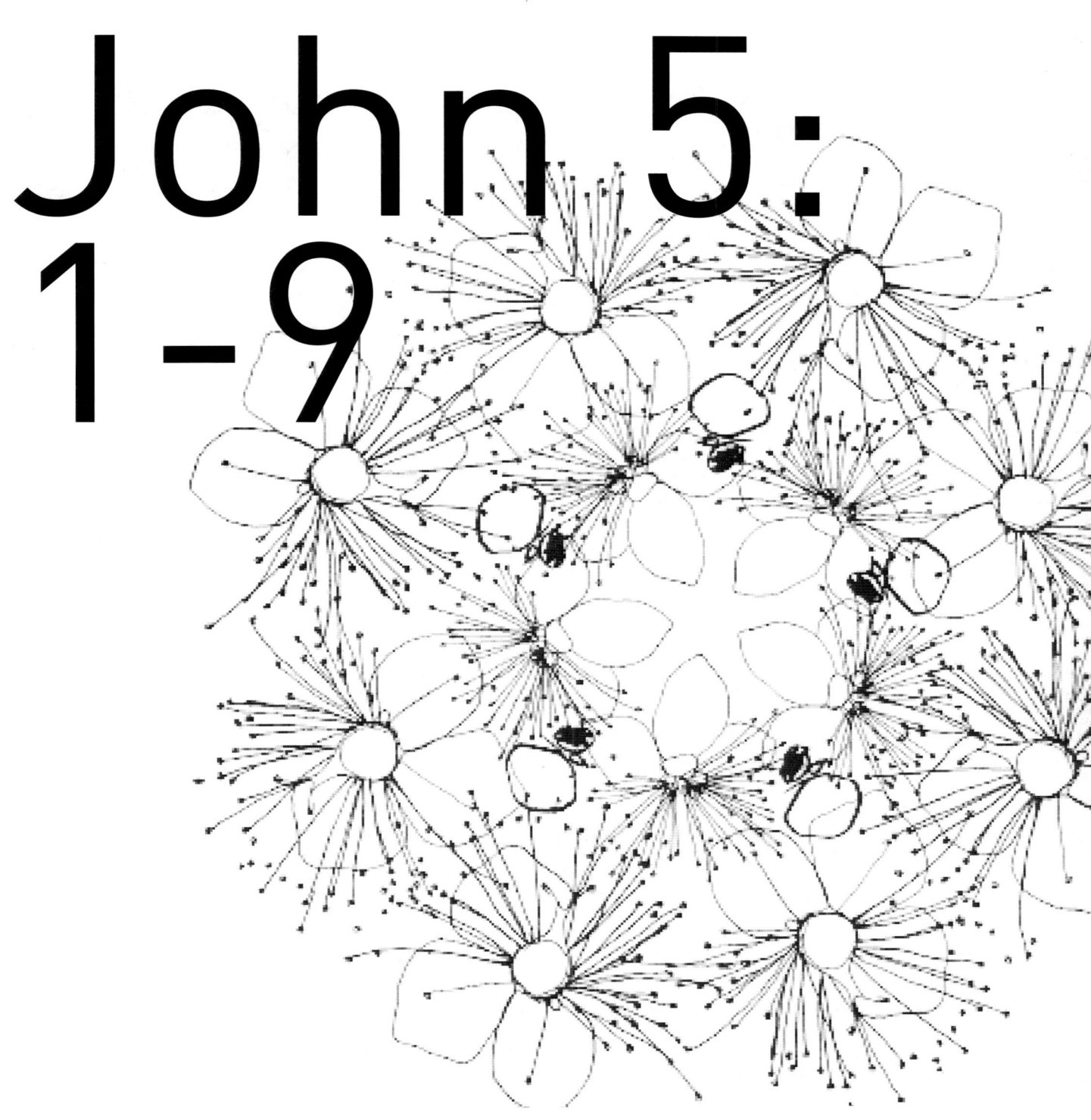

SUM
MER

Hypericum androsaemum
Tutsan

"Derived from the French 'toute-saine' meaning 'all healed' or 'all healthy,' Tutsan has long been used as an antiseptic for flesh wounds."

13 Poolside
(John 5:1-9)

Today's Gospel reading is, for me, nothing
short of amazing. I am
quite literally dumb
founded when I read this text. It is an extraordinary story about an extraordinary encounter
by a pool of water near to one of the gateways into Jerusalem.

We may imagine it how we like, really:
quite ornate with its five porticos or archways, and steps going down into the water;
or something rather grand you'd find in a great stately garden;
a natural feature, cut out of the living rock, with slippery ledges, uneven—quite dangerous;
or else rather more like a country pond with sloping sides where the sheep going into the city for slaughter could pause
for a final farewell drink.

But a pool of water it was—very ancient, with stories about its magical healing properties
going back generations. A pool
where, every so often, little eddies and whirls appeared unannounced,
(like those bubbles you see in streams when the fish dart up to take a passing fly). A pool

of water around which gathered the sick, those with bad backs, and aching muscles,
those with fevers and internal diseases,
those who couldn't afford the local physicians,
or had no health insurance,
those who suffered from long-term illnesses for which there were no known cures;
the hopeless cases, the forgotten ones, those abandoned by all decent law-abiding folk,
those whose only solace lay in a swift and merciful death. Just imagine!

And one man in particular—just one of the many there as Jesus passed.
One of the nameless-ones, who had spent his life hoping against hope. Thirty-eight years of waiting, of
lying there, of
desires dashed
when the crowd stampeded to get into the pool
(if and when the breath of God stirred the waters). Thirty-eight years:
a wasted life. Thirty-eight years
and a prostrate future stretching out before him into a living nightmare. Thirty-eight years;
just imagine! The story

is a wonderfully simple one.
Jesus passes by and
perhaps he recognized him from before?
perhaps he spoke to him on a whim?
perhaps he was the only one there, it being the Sabbath? But
Jesus passes by and says: *"Do you want to be made well?"*

The man is flustered and doesn't answer. Instead he starts rambling on about the crowd, and the stampede, and that all his friends have given up and left him there, so he can never get down to the water, and could you spare me some loose change, because I've not...

13 Poolside

"Do you want to be made well?"
Confronted again by the question (the obvious question,
so long awaited, so
sudden, so
simple),
the man is speechless.
Quite unexpectedly, out
of the blue, out
of the ordinary, out
of his mind with longing.
His one desire is there before him.

Never mind that it's not how the script said it should be,
(there were no eddies in the pool just then).
Never mind that it's this odd preacher man asking him
(teasing him? taunting him? tricking him? He wasn't sure);
his one desire is there
before him. There
for the taking. There!
("I just have to reach out. I just have to say yes. And the nightmare is over.")

"Do you want to be made well?"
(The words echoed ominously and strangely potent.)

Then Jesus says:
"Stand up. Stand up! Pick up your mattress and walk. Go on! Get out of here! Go
and show yourself to those friends of yours who abandoned you."

And the man does so. He stands. And finds himself healed. Extraordinary! (Even
for a Sabbath.)

Now all this is very hard work for us.
Hard work: because we are sons and daughters of the rational world.
Hard work: because we are sons and daughters of the Sadducees:
we don't really believe in resurrection, do we?
Hard work: because we are children of the church:
a church that has come to traffic only in small time truth,
a church that has forgotten the big picture about the way God is, and about what Jesus proclaims,
a church that prefers to think about those inconsequential, unimportant, trivial, banal, third-order
things. And pretend there's nothing bigger.

But make no mistake.
Today we have before us a story that announces to us that,
despite all our hard-won knowledge,
the management of our lives is still completely outside our control.

Today we have before us an incident that announces to us the extraordinary possibility that
we have entirely forgotten what God is all about.

SUM
MER

We have before us a "miracle,"
an "odd thing," an anomaly, a very singular singularity;
a thing that we actually find deeply disturbing. That we wish would go away.
For it goes against all we know about nature. Against everything we have come to trust.
Against all our instincts.
Against those experts we see paraded nightly on our TV screens.

We have before us the tale of a man, just like us,
who cannot believe his ears, or
his eyes, or
his senses, or
his mind.
(With no experts of his own to consult!)

The story of a man, just like us,
who is dumbfounded and confused by the offer of unexpected life.

The story of a man who witnesses—in his own routine, run-of-the-mill, life
the resurrection power of God
battering at the door of his mind and his soul,
the resurrection power of God
breaking in, unfolding itself, and touching his flesh-and-blood life ...

Now
we live in a world that seems full of threats: real and actual.
The threat of terrorism,
the threat of global warfare, of environmental disaster, of the uncertainty of GM foodstuffs,
of unemployment, illness, misfortune;
threats of every size and shape and proportion. You name it, we fear it.

And we find ourselves clutching at straws.
To guarantee our future security: we invest
in pensions and insurance, we play
the stock exchange, we spend
money on lotteries and scratch cards, we bury
ourselves in busyness and stress, and
some of us
work overtime
trying to get to heaven.

And yet all the while
we find ourselves unable to see the one threat that really should concern us.
The threat of life!
The threat of life that God holds out to us. (To each and all of us.)

The threat of God's power for life.
The threat of God's resurrection power that counters the vicious cycles of death that
enthrall us.
A resurrection power that will not be overcome, denied, or resisted

13 Poolside

(as our nameless thirty-eight year-old ancestor discovered that day by the pool).
A resurrection power that is not limited to the pages of the Bible:
but that is alive and well and
out there and in here
among us. Yes: even us! And even here!

God's power for life is not a religious fantasy.
It's not just for biblical days,
for Sundays
for charismatic or evangelical churches,
or for those that are popular and packed to the doors.

It's for churches like this one—churches at the crossroads,
churches open to the future,
churches half-empty
of past restraints,
churches half-full
with room for growing,
churches seeking to worship God with a quiet dignity and a love for neighbors and
a deep passion for the community.

God's resurrection power-for-life is real!
And the threat of it, the offer of it, the gift of it
is always there, just before us, just within our grasp. Just
believe it, just reach up, and take it in your hands.
Even on a Sabbath.
Even today. Even now.
Even as Jesus passes amongst us.

Listen!
Look!
What's he saying?
What's that?
What?
Us?
Are you serious?

SUM
MER

Acts 2:1-21; John 14:9-17

Clematis vitalba
Traveler's Joy

"Beggars used to rub the sap of fresh stems and twigs onto their body in order to create the apperance of ulcers and to arouse sympathy."

14 The Holy Spirit who Beggars Belief
(Acts 2:1-21; John 14:9-17)

I used to work with street people in Manchester.
People who choose to live and work on the streets—sex workers of various sorts.
People *who don't choose* to live on the streets, but who are there because life has dealt with them harshly.
And people who have wandered out onto the streets,
in alcoholic or drug- or debt- or panic-induced states and who are never "together enough"
to get themselves back off the streets again. Some

live off charity and hand-outs in order to make ends meet. And some
also *need to beg*—for a variety of reasons that it may be easy for the rest of us
to judge.

And when I walk around the streets of Manchester it saddens me greatly, all these years later, to see some of the same people still there,
still begging,
like they were years ago. Begging beggars.

We all have our own experience of beggars. Some of us
have decided never to give to "those scroungers." Some of us
do—aware that even so we might be being taken for a ride. And some of us
will buy food or hot drinks or bus tickets, instead. But

whether you've worked with beggars
or whether you've just met beggars
on the streets, most of us will know what an encounter with a beggar
"feels like."
Inside us. How we respond at their approach. Beggars!

There they are on the pavement with their blanket and their dog.
(the dog is no gimmick: but perhaps their only loving relationship.)
Or else they may be heading your way, "working" the crowd. Coming straight towards you!
Do you
dart out of the way? Dare you
make eye-contact? Do you give? And
how little?
(And please don't think that, even my experience of working with them makes me in any way invulnerable to these thoughts!)

Encountering beggars can be a risky business. Precarious!
We may risk verbal abuse—as easily as the "have a nice day" catch phrase.
We might imagine a threat or an aggressive gesture.
We might run the danger of having to listen to some endless and highly dubious sob story
or heart-rending real-life tragedy.
We might even risk being deflected from our intention that day: being late for
that meeting, that show, or that piece of business. We might even,
if we're slow enough,
gullible enough,
brave, or stupid enough,
socially minded, or Christian enough, find ourselves

entering their world,
and coming to see the world through their eyes
and, in the process,
find our lives changed for ever.

After all, it happened to me.
The direction of my ministry and Christian practice was turned
upside
down,
and inside
out.
And my faith was, quite literally, beggared. My belief was beggared!
Imagine that!

I sat with them behind dustbins and under arches.
I came to share their stories, lives, and food; their sorrows and joys, triumphs and defeats.
I admired their resilience, their tenacity and, often, their crafty cunning.
I tried to fathom the depths and chasms of their personal woundedness (and
I let them help me with my own).

And, despite the occasional violent flaring of frustrated anger,
I wondered at their understanding of each other's fragility
and the way in which, often in such abject wretchedness,
gallows humor, mixed with gentleness and patience,
could bring an inner strength and hope.
Enough, at least, for another day's living.

In my experience
the action of the Holy Spirit, also called—strange name—Paraclete
(poured out upon disciples
then and now:
the Sprit of the living God we celebrate this Pentecost day)
can be likened to the action of a beggar.

The Spirit of God, this Paraclete
that is in each one of us
(whoever we are, however "holy" or else "unworthy" we imagine ourselves to be)
this Spirit of the living God
is just like a beggar!

Think about this next time you meet one in the street. Like a beggar!

For the Spirit too is persistent with us, persevering, relentless, and resolute;
insisting on getting our attention, our response, our reaction;
determined to make eye- heart- wallet- and soul-contact.

Like a beggar the Spirit is creative-cunning,
inventive-resourceful,
challenging our values and self-definitions, testing our limits,

meeting us at the edges of our experience and
drawing us on, out, up, and beyond ourselves,
teasing us across our settled horizons,
coaxing us down unfamiliar alleyways and
revealing herself to us!

Like a beggar, the Spirit of God is no respecter of persons:
just as keen to approach the expensive suit, the short skirt, or the threadbare anorak;
always there trying to tap us for what we're reluctant to give,
always looking for unexpected ways to take us for a ride,
always unpredictable,
risky, dangerous, life-threatening, death-defying,
like a leap into the darkness.

Not wanting to un-nerve us completely, however,
this living Spirit also sometimes approaches and draws close to us
with a welcoming smile on her face!

Persuading us to give up our gifts
with familiar words and catch phrases
designed to seduce us to compliance:

"Do not be afraid."
"I call you by your name—you are mine."
"You are precious in my sight."
"You are redeemed. Go free."
"And love one another—as you are loved."

So how do we respond when this beggarly Spirit approaches us?
Can we look upon her gaze?
Do we try to dodge her - and hide anonymously in our crowded lives and busyness?
Do we give of ourselves? And how much can we afford?
Just the small change of our lives?
Or something more substantial?

Do we dare say yes to the life-changing words and gestures proffered by this beggarly Spirit?
Do we take the risk of placing ourselves
into the hand of the One whose holy work sustains us all?
This Holiest of Beggars.
This Helper and Comforter.
This Advocate.
This—strange word—Paraclete.
Do we dare?
Go on now. I dare you.
Dare you.
Dare you?

[Oh, and you do know, don't you, what that strange word "Paraclete" means in modern Greek?
Why, "beggar," of course!]

Acts 2:1-21; John 20:19-23

Roadside flowers

15 On the Road Again

(Acts 2:1-21; John 20:19-23)

"How is it that we hear [them] in our own native language?"

This is one of the most foundational texts in the New Testament:

God giving the disciples the power to speak in multiple tongues
(just like that; in an instant!)
and in the various languages
(just like that; in an instant!)
of all those present in Jerusalem that day: so that all might hear the Good News.
(Just like that; in an instant. And as a linguist I'm more than very envious!)

"How is it that we hear [them] in our own native language?"

It's always struck me as significant that the Spirit gives the disciples the power
of language, speech, and communication.

Why not the power to astonish—with miracles and mighty deeds of healing?
Why not the power to feed the gathered crowds—by multiplying loaves of bread and fishes?
Why not make it clear to the world that these disciples had the same amazing gifts as Jesus?

But what's given that day is the one gift that
was needed for that
particular time, and that
particular place.
The one gift that would enable news of the Good News to break out of its backwater breech
its backyard confines, and begin
to cross its frontiers: out into the bigger world beyond.
The gift of language, speech, and communication is the one gift that was utterly
essential.

The crowd's response (predictably perhaps)
is confusion, mixed
with radical amazement and astonishment. Not new wine talking, but a new vision dawning.
A future suddenly opening up
out of the finality of crucifixion, death, and despair.

And then, suddenly,
quite unexpectedly, they're off;
they're on the road again, those first disciples. But where would it lead them? And what
would they encounter on the wayside?

Now let's pull over for a moment, you and me. Let's take five minutes to consider things. To pack a few necessaries for the journey and study our own road maps. Any history book, travelogue, or sci-fi film will remind us that a fascination with journeying and adventure has always been central to human identity. And the Christian faith is one that is radically oriented towards the future. Indeed we often talk of our discipleship in terms of a journey. Jesus—and now the disciples—are all people on a journey. Just like us!

Journeying
into strangeness, newness, and difference,
with fear-and-curiosity-mixed-in-equal-measure,
offers us a pretty elemental experience:
a thrill, a frisson, a quivering and a quaking to grab us viscerally, in our guts.
(not to mention a few exotically-colored butterflies fluttering around inside us).

For crossing boundaries and frontiers requires us to risk what is familiar and safe,
and discovering
the routes and pathways that allow us to cross back and forth over the boundary
between what is safe and secure and what is perilous and risk-filled;
between what-is and what-is-yet-to-be.

A similar openness to risk and to the unknown is demanded of those of us who would be spiritual
wayfarers and soul travelers.
(Especially perhaps those of us who see ourselves as would-be disciples.)

And it is very often the case that the distance from our head
to our
heart, from
hearing to responding, from
dreaming the destination to actually setting off,
is far greater than even the vast journeys across our continents and oceans that we sometimes
undertake for pleasure or for business. Frequently, however,
spiritual journeys can take a life time. But
fortunately for us, that's exactly the length of time we have available!

Now what Peter is inspired to communicate with his new-found linguistic skills,
as he and the others set off on the road, adventuring,
is the ancient text of the prophet Joel.
A text that Jesus himself had never used.
A text that tells that of the outpouring of God's Spirit.
A text that puts into a cultural context the scale of the astonishing things that God is doing.
A text that serves to prize open their minds
(theirs and ours) to the radical amazement that's needed to begin to comprehend the magnitude
of what God is doing.

For many centuries these two texts—Joel and Acts—have been regarded largely as historical curiosities;
referring only to their own time and meaningful only for those who heard them
back then. (They are just "back then" texts. In the Bible—and, therefore of no practical, earthly use, you
understand!)

This is very bad theology, as I hope you all recognize! For I know that
you know that wherever and whenever scripture is proclaimed
the Spirit of God is alive,
moving among us,
cajoling us, making us curious,

15 On the Road Again

urging us to respond, daring us to say yes to God's call.
Those early disciples around Jesus imagined that the crucifixion was the end. It wasn't. Because the totally unexpected happened!
And Peter was struggling not to be blown away by it all.
And perhaps we are too. (Or should be!)

Yet the totally unexpected is always happening, for God is
a God of new life, of unexpected beginnings and fresh starts.
And though many of us choose to live with the idea that God is a "back then" God,
(a tired gray-haired old man in the clouds, who is fast losing interest and teeth),
the reality, that we celebrate each Sunday, is
that we are always and forever
bidden to get up,
shake off the dust from our bodies, and carry on traveling.

For God is forever taking ancient dusty texts, and unlikely people,
and calling us to new life.
God is forever giving us the gifts, the skills, the attitudes and imagination
needed for right here and for right now. Gifts for the journey that starts afresh each day.

Today's world is a very different place from "back then."
But it's just as confusing, just as trouble-filled, and just as full of woes and joys.

Yet just as Jesus breathed the Spirit on those first disciples,
(just as God had breathed the Spirit into Adam and Eve in the garden, we read)
so the same Spirit is alive for us.
Right here and right now!

For God never ceases
to call us, never ceases
to recreate and remake us, never ceases
to urge us on, up, out, further, never ceases
to dare us to take risks,
to step outside our comfort zones, our familiar backyards, and
those little boxes in which we love to hide. God

ever bids us cross the next horizon, and the one after that; calling us
to be the difference that we ourselves would like to see; calling us
to let go, and reach out, and touch the divine that is within us and around us; calling us
to new life, new hope, and new vision.
Even me. Even you, Even now. Calling us
to the performance of our life time. Can you
sense the Spirit moving? Listen. Can you
hear that still small voice calling you, each in your own language and tongue? Listen. Then
say yes.
Say yes, and set off in pursuit. Listen.
And prepare to be astonished.

SUM
MER

1 Samuel 15:34–16:13; Mark 4:26–34

Woodland fungi

16 Where Do You Go to Find God?

(1 Samuel 15:34-16.13; Mark 4:26-34)

Tell me, please, where do you go to find God?
And, when you get there, tell me, do you recognize him?

Here's a sermon for all you fans of Pooh Bear. It begins like this.

"[One day] Christopher Robin said, 'What do you like doing best in the world, Pooh?'
'Well,' said Pooh, 'what I like best—' and then he had to stop and think ... and ... when he had thought it all out, he said, 'What I like best in the whole world is Me and Piglet going to see You, and You saying 'What about a little something?' and Me saying, 'Well, I shouldn't mind a little something, should you, Piglet, ... it being a hummy sort of day outside, and the birds singing.'

"'I like that too,' said Christopher Robin, 'But what I like doing best is doing Nothing.'
'How do you do Nothing?' asked Pooh, after he had wondered a long time.

"'Well, it's when people call out to you, just as you are going off to do it, 'What are
you going to do, Christopher Robin, and you say Oh, nothing, and then you go and do it.'
'Oh, I see,' said Pooh.

"'This is a nothing sort of thing that we're doing now,' [said Christopher Robin].
'Oh, I see,' said Pooh again.
'It means just going along, listening to all the things you can't hear, and not bothering.'
'Oh,' said Pooh.

"They walked on, thinking of This and That, and by-the-by they came to an enchanted place on the very top of the forest ... . And by-and-by Christopher Robin came to an end of [his thoughts] ... and was silent, and he just sat there looking out over the world, and wishing it wouldn't stop." [8]

Tell me: where do you go to find God?
And, when you get there, how do you recognize her voice?

The prophet Samuel went to Ramah, to his special place.
He sat down on a log and listened.
It's what he did best, listening.
He could listen
all day long and wish it would never stop. He listened
to God. It's even what his name meant. Samuel: the God listener.

And where ever he went people would say:
"Better watch out for him. He's dangerous. He's a troublemaker, that God listener!"
(For listening to God, and then trying to pass on the message, can be surprisingly difficult.
And he didn't always get it right)

Now Samuel listened: long and hard. And he knew in his bones
that something was happening in the world.

But when Samuel thought he heard God suggesting Saul to be king, things had all gone
dreadfully sour and pear-shaped,
for even though Saul did look every inch a king and not at all pear-shaped
he turned out to be very sour indeed.
And that was partly the problem.

SUMMER

[8] A.A. Milne, *The House at Pooh Corner* (New York: Dutton Children's Book, 1988) p.172-176.

Now, though, when Samuel listened again,
he thought he heard God telling him to get up and have another go.
"Choose another king. And try to get it right this time!"

So Samuel sat on his log and listened.
"Go to Bethlehem," God continued.
"Pretend you're going to worship. Take a cow to sacrifice. Don't let those awful locals put you off.
Just go. Be brave!"
But Samuel was uneasy and surprisingly lacking in confidence, (for a professional God-listener).
"Suppose I go there," he thought, "will I recognize the man God wants for king this time?"

And perhaps we can sympathize with his dilemma
for, where do *you go* to find God?
And when you get there, how do you recognize God's voice?

In Bethlehem a certain Jesse lined up his several sons. Which one
would God choose for king?
Not Eliab—big and tough.
Not Abinadab—tall and very fit.
Not Shammah—good with livestock.
Not any of the first seven fine strapping sons Jesse brought out.

In the end the somewhat desperate Jesse called in his youngest, David.
He was ruddy, and handsome, and had such beautiful eyes.
But how could Samuel be sure God wanted this one? Until
a voice in his head, and a familiar feeling in his guts, confirmed to him God's choice.

God had chosen
the youngest and the smallest: upsetting the apple-cart of people's expectations. But
Samuel the God-listener had learned through experience
never to be surprised by God.
He had learned that God rarely speaks in entirely predictable ways.
He had learned that the knack of listening to God was to open up his heart and mind
to the unthinkable:
and be prepared to imagine the unimaginable.
"Always let God surprise you," his old teacher Eli had counseled.

So tell me, *where do you go* to find God?
And when you get there, how do you recognize what she has to show you?
How do you respond? With your mind closed to anything too risky or challenging?
With your expectations held tightly in your hands and behind your back?
Determined that God Will Not Budge You from your habits-of-a-lifetime?

Christopher Robin sat in his enchanted forest listening to all the things he couldn't hear;
but listening all the same.
Samuel the God-listener sat on his log,
listening hard

16 Where Do You Go to Find God?

as the voice of God turned his assumptions upside-down. And now...

Jesus sat on the sea-shore, his very special place, listening to his disciples.

All day long they had watched as Jesus taught the crowds,
and now—alone with him,
at last—they were bursting
with questions. Jesus had talked
about God and about God's kingdom. Not a magical land or fantasy Pooh-bear world,
where wishes all come true
not a place as such, at all!: but a way of living.
God's way of living.

And now there they were on the sea-shore, of all places;
listening, and watching, and trying hard to recognize God in the midst of them,
listening, and watching, and trying hard to understand what Jesus was telling them.

"God's kingdom is like ...
is like ...
is like ..." (Jesus thought long and hard about what to say. He was often better at wood than words.)
"It's like the seed that a farmer sows on his land.
He scatters it and ... Hey presto ... it comes to life by itself. Imagine that!
Tiny seeds producing a great harvest ... Completely unexpected!

"Or else it's like ...
a mustard seed. Tiny, tiny, tiny: yet turning into a huge bush.
Do you see what I'm saying?"
Jesus looked around at his disciples.
They were listening so hard. Watching so hard. Trying so hard
to open up their minds.

"The kingdom of God is never what you'd
expect it to be. It's never how and where you'd
imagine it to be. God is not what you
think. You
have to open up your
minds and lay aside your
assumptions. Look for the unexpected. And use your
imagination!'

And by-the-by Jesus came to and end of his thoughts, and was silent.
He just sat there looking out over the world, wishing it would never end.
And how his disciples wished he would never stop speaking!

Samuel, Jesus, his disciples, (even Christopher Robin, and Pooh),
all of them
looking for God in their own ways,
and in the places where they find themselves.
They don't have to go anywhere. And nor do we.

SUMMER

For God is under our very noses. Closer
to us than we are to our very selves!
Do we expect to find an old gray-haired man sitting on a cloud? Forget it!
Do we expect to find God up in heaven pulling on the strings of our destiny? No way!
Do we expect God to send down lightning, and plagues, and disasters on the people we don't like?
Think again! God

is more than any of us can imagine. And God
is always beyond what we can conceive. We think we've got God
pegged and—no! For God
is always different, always more, always beyond, always ahead. And yet
always right under our noses.

So where do we go to find God?
And when we get there, how do we recognize his calling us?

Well, there are no magical enchanted forests. There's just
the here-and-now, just us living our lives as we move forever on
to what comes next. Just
those many passing moments which, if we try to seize them, slip effortlessly
through our fingers. But God is
among us. God is
here. Here
in our struggles to love as best we can. Here
in our struggles to overcome our selfishness and insecurity and to build a better world. Here
in our struggles to let go of the things that scare us, shame us, cower us, and
stop us being creative and life-transforming. Here. So

let's start listening to God, here inside ourselves.
Let's start believing that we're okay—and that we matter,
Let's start taking risks and make a real difference in the world.
Let's start imagining that life never ends—and discover that it's really so.
Let's dare to lay aside our old assumptions;
and say yes to the longing we feel inside us.
Let's listen, and watch, and try
to see how the Spirit of God is speaking to us even now;
in our own ways, and in the places where we find ourselves.

We don't have to go
anywhere!
Just let's open our eyes and...

1 Kings 19:1-15a; Luke 8:26-39

SUMMER

Viola tricolor
Heartsease

"It has long been used to treat chest complaints, bronchitis and whooping cough."

17 Voices

(1 Kings 19:1-15a; Luke 8:26-39)

What are you doing here, Elijah,
lying under a broom tree, far from home?
What are you doing here?
Who are you fleeing? Why are you afraid?"

The memory of the past days fills Elijah's mind again.
And that message from Queen Jezebel, threatening his death.
He shudders. Caught up in an uncontrollable whirlwind of dread.

"Take a little food and drink," the angel said.
Then Elijah finds himself driven out again into the wilderness.
For forty days and forty nights he marches. High up in the hill country. Far
from human contact.
"What are you doing here, Elijah, so far

from home? Flash forward a thousand years, and
Jesus is far from his home,
high up in the hill country. Well beyond the safety
of familiar Jewish territory.

"What have you to do with me?" the madman asks him.
"What are you doing here, Jesus?
What do you want with me? Go away."

Two stories separated by a millennium.
Two stories about two people far from their homes. Elijah
and Jesus:
on the far side of safety.
Well outside their comfort zone. Dis-located. Wary.

Two stories with a disturbing, dream-like, quality. Nightmarish, even.
Like King Lear on his windswept moor in the dead of night: lamenting, regretting, moaning, wishing
things were other than they are.
And that's the clue, the link. Their commonality.
And ours, perhaps?

The 3 am blues! Do you get them?
Often in the wee small hours, I awake.
Perfectly happy when I went to bed. And sleeping soundly.
But now they emerge. Out of the cracks of my dreaming:
the doubts, the questions, the nagging fears.
The demons of the night!
Do they visit you too?

Some of our fears are real enough, of course. But many more are just imaginary.
We may drown them out by day with our busyness, our thinking of other things; but they emerge
at night
to roam around our semi-conscious minds when our mental guard is off duty.

We toss and turn to try and shake them off.
But they wake us, nonetheless, with their scuttling. Scuttling. Irrational
fears. Niggling
doubts, about nothing in particular: taunting me.
Noisily rearranging the mental furniture in my half-awake brain. Disturbing
my rest. Prodding
at my tranquility with their sharp questions: What
are you doing here? When
are you going to get your life together? Who
are you fleeing? Where
are you? Why
are you afraid? What
is the matter with you? What
do they want with me?
Filling my head, those voices that refuse to be silenced.

*Witness poor Elijah caught up in that nightmare whirlwind of fear, staggering
to stand upright during that dread earthquake. Covering
his face with that famous mantle to block it all out.
And then
calm. Stillness and silence.
At the coming of God. When, inside his head, he hears
the voice of God speak.*

*Witness too the so-called demoniac.
So many voices in his head! Like a legion marching through his brain.
Thousands of them! And all talking at once!
Stifling him. Possessing his being with their endless babbling!
The chaos of the man's mind is visible as he writhes, pulling,
pulling, pulling,
on his chains amongst the jagged rocks of the graveyard.
And then
calm. Stillness and silence.
At the coming of the Lord. When Jesus
speaks.*

God calms the raging chaos around Elijah, calling out
his inner fears and dread, just as Jesus calls out
the legion of voices from the man's mind,
overruling the demons that torment him.

For the voice of God is restorative and recreative. And
just as God speaks at the dawn of time, calling each creature into life,
just as the voice of God brings life to the dead,
speaking Easter in a garden on that First Day of the week, so
the voice of God brings life: life
to those whose world is chaotic and disordered, life
to those whose hearts, and souls, and minds are disintegrating, life
to those whose ability to hope is drowning under a rising tide of self doubt, cynicism, or despair.

And that life-
bringing voice of God is all around us:
saturating our world with its recreative love
overflowing any bounds and limits that we might create. And be assured that this is so.

The recognition of this voice,
as by Elijah on the mountain top,
as by the disturbed man in the graveyard,
is deeply healing, calming, forgiving, and restoring…

At the end of his story
Elijah's fear is banished, his calm is restored, and he's sent back to complete his prophetic mission.

At the end of his story
the so-called demoniac is clothed and in his right mind.
He too is sent back to where he belongs: to his family and his home. He is restored.

And that same experience of restoration is available for us. Whenever
our heart is overwhelmed, whenever
our mind is confused, whenever
our soul feels bruised and hurt. The trick
is to be still, as still
as we can, or like, or dare;
to become aware
of the loving presence of God all around:
closer to us than we are to our very selves,
(consider that some time, please);
and to hear the voice of God
raising us up with love.

Our mind's, and soul's, and heart's ease.

Exodus 16:13-21; John 6:51-58

SUM
MER

Triticum
Wheat

"There are over 30,000 different species of wheat grown throughout the world"

18 Just a Pinch of Revelation

(Exodus 16:13-21; John 6:51-58)

> *"'I am the living bread that came down from heaven ...*
> *Those who eat my flesh and drink my blood abide in me and I in*
> *them.' He said these things while he was teaching in the synagogue*
> *in Capernaum."* (John 6:51, 56, 59)

Some people read recipe books at bed-time since,
they say, recipes have guaranteed Happy Endings (Always. In the books at least!).
They say it helps them sleep better. Well,
what I have for you to day is really more recipe than sermon. So let's
see what we can make with it: and whether or not it sends you off to sleep!

First take a pinch of revelation.
Last week I had a small revelation
(right here! Though I don't think anyone noticed.)

Since more of you came to church than were expected,
I had to make the bread
go further amongst more people.
It was home-made bread, good-textured, with lots of air between the bread particles. But
I had to stretch it out. So some
of you got the usual amount. Some
got half the usual amount. Some
got just a little. And
by the time I received my communion, right at the end, there was just a tiny piece left over.
You could hardly pick it up.
It was just a couple of particles of bread:
with more air-in-between-than-substance; more space-between-the-bread
than bread itself.
(Can you imagine that?)

And it was then that
I had the curious revelation, that,
had there been no bread left at all, but only the air from in-between the bread particles,
then it would still have been Holy Communion,
still have been the Bread of Life.
Can you see what I'm getting at? That
bread isn't just the substance, the particles, the crumbs;
but the space in between as well: that
there's more to bread than just bread. (And always has been.)

"He said these things while he was teaching in the synagogue in Capernaum.
'I am the living bread,'" he said. But what did he mean?

Next add water and yeast, and a pinch of salt. Or something.
In the wilderness Jesus
first fed the Four Thousand,
then he did it again with Five Thousand.

18 Just a Pinch of Revelation

(Just to make a point and to stretch the bread a bit further.
You can read these recipes in Matthew, Mark, and Luke.) But
He used a traditional technique, with a modern twist to give it new life:
an ancient recipe from that royal cookery book called Second Kings It goes like this.

"*A man came from Baal-shalishah, bringing food from the first fruits to [Elisha], the man of God:
twenty loaves of barley and fresh ears of grain in his sack.
Elisha said, 'Give it to the people and let them eat.'
But his servant said, 'How can I set this [tiny amount] before a hundred people?'
So [Elisha] repeated, 'Give it to the people and let them eat, for thus says the L*ORD*, 'They
shall eat and have some left.'
He set it before them, they ate, and had some left, according to the word of the L*ORD
(2 Kings 4:42-44)."

Did you recognize that?
Jesus used the yeast of that story for his own bread-making in the wilderness. (Adding
a few fishes as a garnish.) But
on *this* memorable day in the synagogue in Capernaum he told them the story of an
exotic,
desert recipe,
passed down to him (on his father's side):

Wandering in the wilderness, the Israelites all got a bit stale on a diet of roots and seeds.
They longed for the Good Fresh Food they'd grown themselves back in Egypt.
Melons, aubergines, cucumbers, cooked with oil and garlic.
They drooled
at the memory and moaned,
and moaned,
until God sent a miracle. And
at dawn one day the desert floor was carpeted with:
"But what is it?" they asked. (Only they said it in Hebrew: "manna? manna?") And
My! How good it tasted with the quail.
(Even without the garlic.)

Then knead the mixture.
Turning and turning it. Folding
and folding it. Stretching and
stretching it—as far as it will
go.
To let the air in.

In John's gospel Jesus takes all these same ingredients and recipes and
turns them, and
folds them, and
stretches them still further. Giving
a thoroughly contemporary and daring twist to the recipe that took everyone's breathe away.

For Jesus says that he himself is the bread.
The breadmaker has become bread!

SUM
MER

Now Jesus knew a lot about bread. Always had done. It was in his blood, you see.
Jesus was his mother's pride,
born in a town whose very name (Bethlehem: "the house of bread") bore
witness to its location in the heart of the flat plains of Galilee
where the wheat grew down to the lakeside. But
to say that he himself was like a loaf of bread,
like the flat chapattis
the women cooked at home. Well, what exactly did he mean?

The congregation fell silent
that day in the synagogue in Capernaum. They
waited on his
words: waited, waited, waited.

Next leave the dough to rise in a warm place.
Let's sit down and have a break. Take time out to reflect on things, while the dough is rising.

John's gospel is different from the others: written later and in a much more complex way.
The simple bread recipes of Matthew, Mark, and Luke become
a rich and multi-layered confection.

John says things that have more than several meanings and even though, before,
bread always meant more than just bread, now
the recipe has even more possible variations. And so when Jesus says "I am the bread of life,"
we don't quite know
what he really meant: the original version of the text being lost. "I am the bread of life"
could just as easily mean "God is the bread of life."
(For in Hebrew the only way to say "God is"—without pronouncing the Sacred Name
is to say: "I am is." And the actual name of God—Yahweh—means
"I am," or "I am who I am," or "I am being itself."
See how multi-layered this recipe has become!)

Now when the dough is in the oven—turn up the temperature.
The congregation pondered these words. They'd heard Jesus talk before and liked the way he
challenged them to think. But
was he really saying that he and God—and bread—were
somehow the same thing? Was Jesus stretching things too far: even for even this audience?

As they pondered, the room became unbearably hot, and some of them shuffled
uncomfortably. *"I am the living bread,"* he said.

When the mixture becomes good and wholesome bread —turn it out on a plate.
Happily for us, whichever way we make the recipe, the result is more than satisfactory.
For bread (brown, white, granary, chapatti, naan and pitta, baguette, pain de campagne,
Schwarzbrot, and the best homemade)
is the stuff of life.

Knowing about bread
is the simplest recipe for learning about God, the essence

18 Just a Pinch of Revelation

of everything that exists. Understanding bread
is understanding what made Jesus tick. What
gave him his flair for transforming the ordinary into the miraculous.

Jesus took the everyday things of God: the stuff of life, and
using the same ancient recipes known from times long past,
transformed it—with an ever fresh imagination—into living bread that feeds us
symbolically, metaphorically, physically,
with words of life, words
that are, quite simply, good enough to eat,

Finally—take it and eat it just as you like it.
Eat
your fill. Eat
to your soul's content.
Take it and bake it, and bless it, and break it. Eat
it and rejoice.
The bread of life: here for you.
Now.

He said these things while he was teaching in the synagogue in Capernaum.
"I am the living bread," he said. What did he mean?

Come, now—taste, and see and eat.
A recipe to die for!

SUM
MER

Deuteronomy 30:15-19; Luke 10:25-37

Bromus erectus
Upright Brome

"Upright Brome is commonly found on wasteland and roadsides towering over other plants."

19 Choosing Life
(Deuteronomy 30:15-19; Luke 10:25-37)

"Wanting to justify himself, he stood up to test Jesus."

Even though—according to Jesus—the lawyer was doing everything right,
he wanted to justify himself.
He wanted to hear that he was right,
that he was upright and outstanding, (waiting there for Jesus on the roadside)
that he was good,
that he was holy and, most of all,
that he was destined for heaven; for eternal life.
He wanted Jesus to confirm it.
(Preferably in the hearing of as many people as possible.)
Then he would feign to shrug it all off, with great modesty,
and an "Oh! It was nothing very much at all!"

So: game, set, and match! Eternal life here he comes!
All those years of studies!
All the sacrifices he'd made to get where he was!
How the lawyer must have been delighted
to hear Jesus' response: "You have given the *right answer*; do this, and you will live."

Now does that strike any chords with you at all?
It certainly does with me.
For I think I probably spent a great deal of time and effort,
throughout my childhood, my teens, and my early career,
rather desperately engineering situations where someone
(parents, family, teachers, or bosses) would say to me:
"Well done! That's
the right answer! That's
the accurate response! That's
the correct behavior! That's
the very thing we were looking for!!"
And I guess that sometimes I'm probably still playing the same game now. Sad, isn't it?

But, of course, Jesus' initial answer to the lawyer isn't
his last word. For Jesus sees
the game the man is playing. He sees
how he's after high praise and congratulations. He sees
how the man wants to show off. He sees
how he wants to test Jesus, make him squirm a bit perhaps; possibly even catch him out. So he asks.
"Who is my neighbor, preacher man?"
And back comes Jesus, with possibly the most famous story in the Gospels: the "good" Samaritan.

But we need to understand that the lawyer man is doing no more than most of us do, most of the time.
He's wanting affirmation. He's wanting
to be right. He's wanting
to be "found righteous before God."

So let's have some sympathy for him, please! Because
most of us are no better and no worse than he is.

For we're pretty much all wanting
the same thing.

Now. Knowing you all know the story of the "good" Samaritan, inside-out-and-back-to-front,
I'll just skip on down to the punch line, when Jesus asks :
which one was the real neighbor?
Which one of them was the "good" Samaritan?
Which one of us is the "good" Christian?

The answer, on the face of it, is straightforward: it's the one who showed mercy!
Showed mercy, eh? Is it that simple? Really? Surely not! Showing mercy
is the answer? Showing mercy
is the key to eternal life?

But has Luke got it right? Or
is it Matthew who,
in his Gospel, says: "to get eternal life we have to be perfect?"

(What do *you* think? Let's have a quick show of hands.
Who thinks getting eternal life is bound up with being perfect?
And who prefers the idea of showing mercy? And who's undecided?

Well: the gospels are clearly undecided. And that means we
have to choose!!! We
have to decide for ourselves whether the point of the religious life is to be perfect, or
to show mercy.) [And it's scary, this having to make a choice.]

Now the lawyer man is very quick
witted. "The one who
showed mercy" he
shouts. "Bingo!" (But in Aramaic, of course...)
"Yes," says Jesus. "You're
right. You're
so right! So
go
and show mercy." Yes!

According to Jesus—it really is that simple. The key
to eternal life is to show mercy. To other people. And
to yourself! Ah.
That's the hard bit. Showing mercy to ourselves!!
As scripture says:
"Today I set before you life and death, blessings and curses. Choose life that you may live long."
Show mercy. Choose
eternal life. Choose
life! Except,
of course, that very often "choosing
life" is quite a tricky thing to do. Very often "choosing
life" is quite impossible

19 Choosing Life

for us. Because so often we can't help ourselves from choosing
the opposite:
the ways of death. Very often "choosing
life" is quite impossible for us.
Because we can't quite believe that the blessings of life really are real
for us. Very often "choosing life"
is quite impossible.
Because we can't quite *believe* we actually have any choice
or say in the matter. So
we stick to what we know. We
shy away from what Walter Brueggemann calls the "threat of life." "Choosing
life" is just too
scary for us.

That's the dilemma this lawyer faces. And it's our dilemma too. So
what are we to do? How
do we choose
life? How?

Well: here are "six top tips" for Trinity Six. Pick which ever one you choose
as a great place to start: One: *Say*
"Yes" to life:
incurably romantic, hopelessly optimistic, and willfully
embracing all the pain, suffering and messiness in the world. Yes! But
it's the only cure and antidote for the riskiness involved in living life to the full. Two: *Learn*

to live in the present moment: day by day and season by season;
it allows us to discover and experience a heightened sense of the mystery, wonder, and enchantment of
"ordinary" daily life and be open to making new and exciting discoveries, unexpected new
things, ideas, relationships, unbidden insights, and astonishing moments of grace. Three: *Be*

sure to rest each day (and not just when we're asleep in bed).
A spiritual life is one which seeks to balance the busyness of our daily routines and the need to rest and
relax our mind, body, and spirit. Never better
encapsulated than in a famous slogan advertising a particular chocolate
bar which, if consumed
daily, the manufacturers argued, "helps you work, rest, and play." Four: *Make*

space in your soul for other people
Start by listening to the needs of those around you. Then make a difference by Five: *Getting*

involved in social justice and helping to put something right somewhere in your world. Six: *Finding*

something to delight your soul. Whatever
is it that delights your soul? Whatever
is it that brings you pleasure and makes you feel really alive? Whatever it is

find it, explore it, share it with others. Urgently. For:
"See—today I set before you life and death," says the Lord. "Choose
life."

Ephesians 4:25—5:2

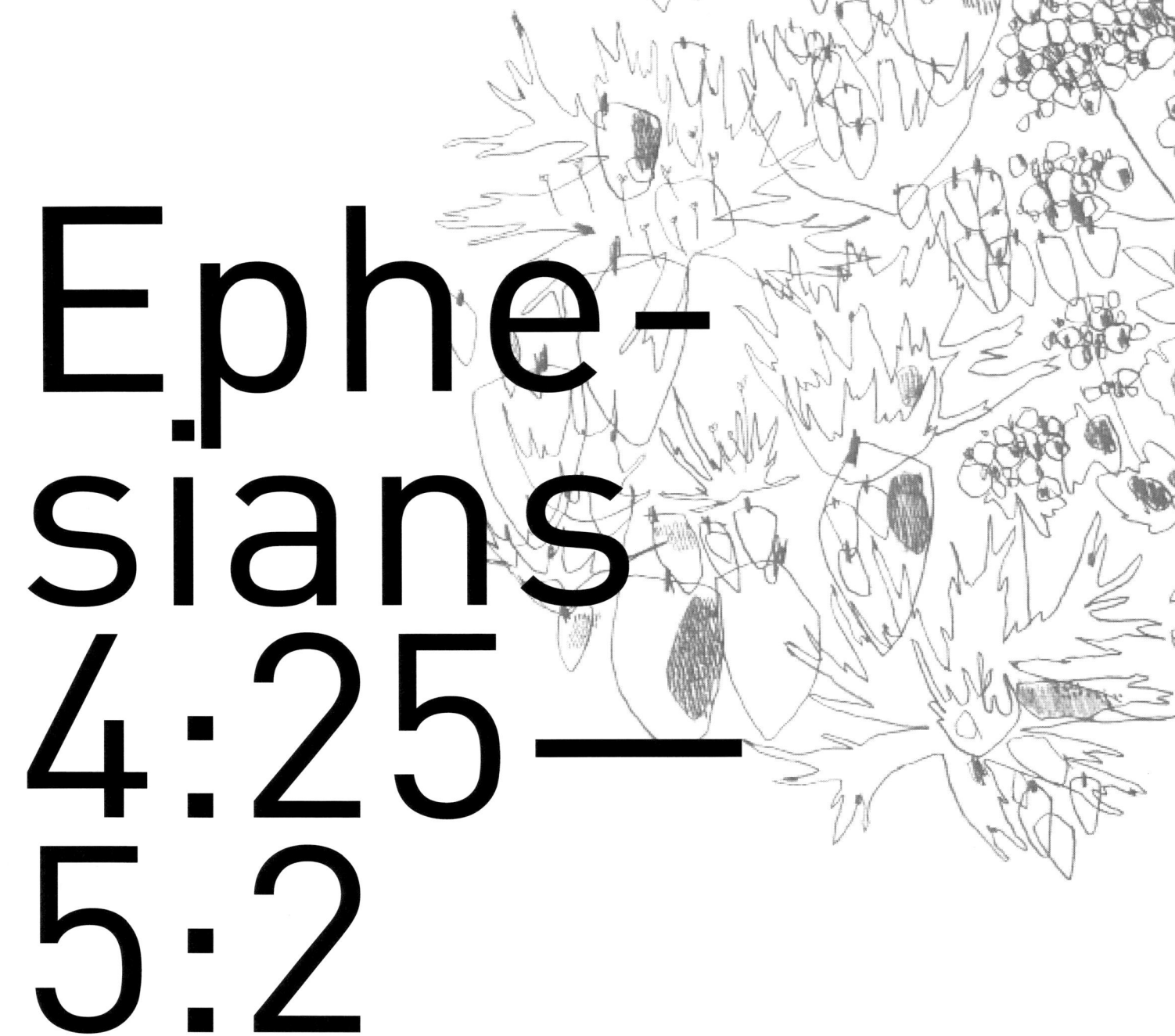

Isatis tinctoria
Woad

Serratula tinctoria
Saw-wort

"Both plants have been extensively used for dying cloth."

20 Divine Falsehood
(Ephesians 4:25-5:2)

"So then, putting away falsehood let us all speak the truth to our neighbors, ... be imitators of God."

In the Middle Ages the clothes you put on in the morning were not a matter of choice.
You put on the clothes that went with your rank, your role, your place in society.
Plain, dark, rough material for
the working classes. Bright, decorated, clothing
for the wealthy. Richly colored, comfortable, textured, designer fabrics
for the nobility.

This was particularly true in the case of your hat—your hood.
Wear the wrong hood
and—well it just wasn't worth taking the risk! Wearing the wrong hood
was actually a crime: and to be arrested for wearing the wrong hood,
to be convicted for the crime of *falsehood*,
could mean a session in the stocks, or a flogging, or worse. Because falsehood
was the worst kind of deception:
deceiving people into believing you were something you were not. Committing falsehood
wearing the wrong hat—imitating your betters—was a crime that struck at the heart of any ordered
society. God forbid! (Best stick to wearing your own hood! And maintain the social *fabric!*) But

scripture tells us to *"be imitators of God."*
A radical thought for the average peasant, back then, going hood-in-hand into church each Sunday
and enviously eyeing-up the clothes the rich folks wore!
And any preacher, back then, who encouraged their congregation to imagine
they were in anyway like God, or were the children of God,
(and so expect, in any sense to be equal to their betters in the real world) ,
soon got their come-uppance! But

scripture still tells us: *"be imitators of God."* Be like God.
And it's still a deeply radical thought for us on a Sunday morning.
Still an idea to threaten society with chaos,
by subverting the social order and bringing down the powers that be:

Be imitators of God. Try God's hat on—just to see if it fits.
Just to see what happens.
Imitate God.
Be as God is.
Do as God does.
See the world like God sees.
Think like God thinks. Go on—give it a go!

Have you ever considered the fact that simply believing in God is a subversive act, these
days?
For many people—perhaps for the majority—belief in God is the supreme
falsehood.
A falsehood
that ought to be punishable in some way; preferably by some kind of very public humiliation in the media.

SUM
MER

Belief in the *real* God is simply not
tolerated. The *real* God:
hidden, unknowable, unimaginable, untamable
with words and images of our own devising, who
can turn the world upside down and inside out, "who
gives life to the dead and who calls into existence the things that do not exist," who
exists to create— and who needs to create in order to exist at all, who
holds the universe in the palm of a hand and sustains everything by calling it and loving it into life,
is *persona non*
grata.

Such a God,
such an ultimate power:
a power beyond that of the US-G8-World Bank-multi-national-global-corporations-and-secret-security-
forces-we-so—revere, is a dangerous madness that
blasphemes
against all the commonly accepted wisdom and sanity of today's world-wide elites.

Of course the old-man-with-a-long-gray-beard-sitting-on-a-cloud-of-fluffy-irrelevance is tolerated; as
a harmless stereotype, *in extremis*, at least.
So too the stern judge who sends down thunder bolts on those *we don't like, or who don't like*
us!
And especially enduring is the vague-as-a-wisp-of-smoke God
whom we shower with our prayers when the cat gets sick, we need a parking space, or the winning
lottery numbers need choosing on a roll-over jackpot weekend.
Most of us prefer this God-of-the-trivial,
this fingers-crossed, touch wood, wishful thinking, just-to-be-on-the-safe-side-God. For

the alternative-real God, who cannot be contained by our own neat and water-tight
definitions, creeds, theologies, and faith systems;
a God who refuses to prefer only people like us,
who think like we think, and who worship like we worship;
a God who sees the world very differently from the way we prefer to do:
such a belief, and such a God is, well, just Not At All Satisfactory, is it? Not
comfortable. It doesn't suit us.

For we all prefer a God of our own making, and of our own choosing.
A God we're snug and cozy with.
After all, if we're meant to be imitators of God—well, we'd rather prefer
to be comfortable in our imitating. Nothing too
demanding or uncomfortable, please!

"Be imitators of God," Paul tells us.
Not at all an easy option, is it?

Not least because the problem with imitating
God, is
that God is
beyond our imagination. Anselm of Canterbury said that God is

20 Divine Falsehood

always greater than we can conceive or imagine. God is always greater than we can imagine. And such a God always requires us to step outside our comfort zone.

We think we have God taped, pinned down in words of black on white, secured on paper, bound in a book (to be taken down off the shelf when the need arises). And we gasp
in frustration when God sets off again, leaping
over that creedal statement, evading
that certainty we thought was set-in-stone, climbing—
Houdini-like—out of those traditions and creeds,
scriptures and theologies we think will forever hold *her*
there, running
on ahead of us as we chase breathlessly behind trying to keep up, allowing
us to spot only lukewarm traces of her recent presence in the words, lines, pages, and chapters of scripture, permitting
us only glimpses in forests and velvety night skies and glorious sunrises,
in silence and in singing, in our stillness and in our love-making,
and in the faces of the starving, the sick, and the dying. So

how are we to imitate God when God is so elusive, evasive, and hard-to-pin-down?
Ought we to lead lives of moral purity to help us imitate God?
Ought we to be perfect in all things to have any chance at all?
Ought we to be so very well-versed in sacred scriptures, knowing it all by heart?
Ought we to spend all our days in prayer, good works, and fasting; scrupulously tithing what we earn?
Ought we to be as utterly selfless as a saint, and humble as a doormat?
Ought we? Ought we? Ought we?
Or would all these "oughts," all this "hardening of the ought-eries," so to speak,
simply bring on an early (and likely terminal) attack of heart and soul-sickness? So

what to do? How is our imitation of this God to proceed? Paul
offers us a clue:
"be imitators of God," he says, "and live in love, as Christ loved us." Imitate God
like Jesus did. Love
like Jesus loved. Go, like Jesus did,
and find those who need to be loved? Yes.
(Do you know someone like that?)
Love those who are loveless, those who are unlovely and unlovable? Yes.
(Do you know someone like that?)
Find those who are despised, rejected, cursed, avoided, shunned? Yes.
(Do you know someone like that?)
Find those who are different and misunderstood? Yes.
(Do you know someone like that?)
Find those who don't fit in to your ways of doing things? Yes.
(Do you know someone like that?)
And then love them. Love them
back to life. Love them
without expecting them
to become like you;
or like how you think
they ought to be.

SUM
MER

And be prepared to risk everything in your loving.
Be prepared to walk further than you imagined in your journey alongside them.
Be prepared for unexpected hardship and to think that all your efforts have been wasted.
Be prepared for that. Love
without conditions. Love
without expecting any warm feelings inside you, when the day is done.
But never stop loving.

For it is in loving, loving beyond all we feel we can bear,
that we might just discover that we ourselves have been loved all along:
loved more than we had ever dared imagine.
And that this love from beyond us— indefinable, indescribable, ever—elusive,
has changed us—softly, secretly, somehow—into
the likeness of the one we thought we were seeking;
but who all the while was seeking us.

Be imitators of God.
Dare yourselves.
Pick up the mantle of God. Put on God's hat. Just to see!
Commit a little divine falsehood.

But watch out.
You may end up being convicted!

Sermons 21-28

AUTUMN

Matthew 16:21-28

Convolvulaceae
Morning Glory

"There are about 1000 types of Morning Glory. All are vines, with saucer-shaped flowers, opening at morning time and closing with the dusk."

21 One Day at a Time
(Matthew 16:21-28) [9]

"Those who want to save their life will lose it." Take up your cross and follow me.

Some of humanity's great steps forward,
some of our greatest discoveries, ideas, and insights
have come in the strangest of places, and at the strangest of times. Archimedes was

having a bath when he discovered the principle of water displacement. Thomas Crapper was
relieving himself when he conceived of the modern flush toilet. Albert Einstein was
having a train ride when he conceived the principle of relativity
Great discoveries and realizations made in the strangest times and places! What about you?

Have you discovered anything lately?
Have you conceived anything wonderful recently?
Have you realized anything important about
your own life or wondered where it's going?
Have you ever asked yourself "is this as good as it gets?"
Do you wake up each morning with anticipation and excitement about what lies ahead?
And go to bed each night with words of thanks in your heart for what the day has held?

Are you enjoying your life? Can you say:
"for all that has been thanks; and to all that's still to come, yes?" Do you
think, if you ever get to those pearly gates, you'll be able to say: "thanks:
I've had a really good time?"

Of course, I don't mean are you partying all the time,
or is your life simply one big round of endless
pleasure: absolute bliss morning, noon and night! No. Enjoying life
is about accepting that
it's not always easy, but it is worth saying yes to it all! Enjoying life

is about accepting there will be difficult times, that
not everything goes our own way, that
life isn't always fair, that
suffering—great and small—is part of the fabric of life.

The snatch of conversation we heard just now between Jesus and Peter is an interesting one.
Peter reckons that if Jesus is who he says he is then, wow!
presumably he could do anything! So
when Jesus talks about pain
and suffering, Peter
suggests Jesus does something about it. "You of all people," he says,
"don't need to have pain and suffering in your life.
Snap your fingers and make with the good times!
Live out your life doing good,
traveling from place to place, healing people, making them happy, and
then live till a ripe old age—and die peacefully in the sun with a glass of wine in your hand."

[9] Dedicated to Jack at his baptism.

(Tempting thought, isn't it.
I once did a funeral for an old lady of eighty, who went on holiday to the sunshine with her family,
had a meal, sat down on the balcony with a brandy to watch the sunset, and died in her chair.
What a way to go! Anyone here for some of that?) But life

isn't like that for most of us, is it? Life
certainly wasn't like that for Jesus. For, you see, at some point in his life,
he'd had a hunch
and the hunch had become an idea, an inspiration, that had given him courage to stake his life
on this hunch-turned-inspiration.

Do you want to know what the hunch was?
(I wonder where he had it: in the bath? sitting under a shady tree with a glass of wine?)
Do you know what his great theory was?

He reckoned that death wasn't everything it was cracked up to be.
He reckoned that you could call its bluff.
He reckoned that you could take it on—and beat it. And
he reckoned that if you did that—why, it would change everything.
It would change the way we look at life.

So that's what he did.
"Those who want to save their life will lose it," he said: to anyone who'd listen. Not
that many did. And, not
knowing whether his hunch would work, or whether it was a totally mad scheme,
he didn't flinch when, one day, soldiers came and arrested him for spreading this mad idea.

He was arrested, had a mock trial, and was nailed to a wooden cross.
(A popular and very effective form of execution, much liked by the occupying forces.)
He died. And then he ... well;
you know the rest of the story. But

that's why today, at Jack's baptism, we will draw with holy oil, a cross
on his forehead. A cross
to show that he belongs to this crackpot community
of people who work very hard at enjoying life: partying
as often as we can, of course,
(and that's why Jack will receive a candle: to help him celebrate life) but
who realize that enjoying life is

about something more.
About accepting that
it's not always easy, but it is worth being here, and saying yes to it all;
about accepting there will be difficult times,
that we will need to say sorry, and start again, and wash the slate clean
(that's why Jack will have water put on his head),
that not everything goes our own way,
that life isn't always fair,

21 One Day at a Time

that suffering—great and small—is part of the fabric of life.
But that death is not what it seems.

And that's a message for everyone.

That the secret of life
is to live it one day at a time;
enjoying the small things, as much as the big things;
enjoying the simple things, as much as extravagance;
enjoying the warmth and intimacy of friendship and love;
relishing the joy to be found in having new life in your midst;
and making fresh discoveries each day
(if we care to look for them)
of beauty, gentleness, kindness, trust, respect, and caring for others.

The secret of life is the curious discovery that these ordinary things
are what and where God is.

I wonder where you'll be,
and what you'll be doing,
when you make this discovery for yourselves.

Enjoy!

AUT
UMN

Mark 9:30-37

Vinca major
Greater Periwinkle

Vinca minor
Lesser Periwinkle

"In medieval England garlands of periwinkles were often worn by those about to be executed, because this evergreen plant was understood to symbolize immortality."

22 Off the Beaten Track

(Mark 9:30-37)

Somewhere-sometime in a forgotten corner of Galilee,
off the beaten track
on a seldom-used back road that wound its way down to Capernaum,
Jesus walked with his disciples,
teaching them as they went along—as he often did.
From time to time the line of men and women spread out, as it often will,
over quite a distance, as Jesus
walked on
alternatively talking and listening, dreaming and praying.

When they eventually arrived at the house in Capernaum,
and had washed, and refreshed themselves with bread and wine,
Jesus asked them what they'd been talking about as they walked along
(and them thinking he was out of ear-shot and all!) Their embarrassed silence spoke
volumes. It seems
the disciples were constantly jockeying
for position.
"Which of us is closest to him?" They asked themselves
"Who's his favorite? They wondered.
"Who is his Indispensable No 1 and Second-Choice No 2?
Who's in-charge when he's away? Who's the trusted deputy?
Is it me? Is it him? Is it her—and she no better than she ought to be!
Who among us is the greatest"?

The story we hear today in Mark is repeated by Matthew and Luke.
And there are other stories too of disciples wanting to be top dog:
James and John wanting seats at Jesus' left and right hand.
(And that same story retold in Matthew's gospel where their poor mother—only a woman!–
is made to take the blame for her sons' ambitions.)
Who among us is the greatest?
Who among us is the greatest?
(Chanted like some playground game.)

And there's no point denying we play the game as well. Just look
around us! There has to be *someone great* here, surely. Some candidate for greatness.
But who is it? Who can it be? And how will we recognize them
and judge?
Should we swap IQ scores—and find the greatest mind? Or shoe sizes, to find the best fit?
Shall we go by age? (But is it greater in our cutting-edge world to be old and full of years—or younger, sexier, and with so much life ahead?)

Should we measure greatness by income— or by charitable giving?
Should we look for obvious signs of holiness— those who've kept all the Ten Commandments? (Hands up! Anyone here owning up to holiness?)
Should we look about us and disqualify those who look a bit shifty, scruffy, and all those wearing trainers or sneakers?
Shall we find out if anyone's been publicly honored? Or are there any heroes? Or those who've worked tirelessly for the community?
Better still: can anyone claim to know, or have met, or touched, some A-list celebrity?

AUT
UMN

And so have prized contemporary value over the rest of us!

How ever we look at it, we're just like those first disciples: seduced
at some deep level of our being by the thought of greatness; tempted
by the prospect of promotion, recognition, advancement, preferment, or
by the lottery of good fortune that might just improve our post- or zip code. And

like those first disciples and early Christians, we inhabit a church that has an unhealthy
pre-occupation with rank and power, prestige and authority
that exactly mirrors the world around us,
instead of reflecting the altogether-upside-down and topsy-turvy reign of God.

Many of us in the church seem to be helplessly addicted
to the need to be righteous and relevant
(and successful at all costs, please; we need the money!),
fascinated with the glamour, the moral imperative, of trying to influence
people's thoughts and lives, behavior and destiny, and so very
desperate to have a "significant" role in the world.

And many of us are so sold on the idea of Jesus as "the greatest person who ever lived,"
(so "completely greater than any other religion's prophet and inspiration"),
that we seem to have forgotten how to live out our lives according to the ordinary, simple goodness of the man himself.

We are so busy shouting that: "Our
God is the greatest," "Our
truth is the greatest," "Our
way of seeing the world is the only one that matters,"
that we seem to have forgotten how to listen to what Jesus himself might have to say.

We have permitted ourselves to be so overcome by fear and insecurity,
so overwhelmed by our lack of moral courage to act decisively in the world
that we have become wholly dependent upon a hero figure, a savior
whose "necessary greatness,"
(our need: not his),
we have allowed to obscure the real message he embodied.

Now, we must think very carefully before we tout ideas of greatness. For what he offers,
is not a popular "recognized high street brand," but
a "down the back-streets" and "off the beaten track" kind of greatness:
tap-rooted in our desire to promote each others' flourishing
and bound up with our ability to nurture each other into becoming
more fully human.

A greatness that concerns itself with encouraging communion between people;
with giving space to each other
by attentiveness and patient listening to each other;
contributing to each other's growth
by creative use of what we receive from each other,

so that we encourage each other
to model the habits and practices of God
in the "this time-" and "this place-ness" of our world:

sensitive collaboration
joint decision-making
flexibility
openness to what is new
a positive willingness to seek opportunities for change
using our imagination to turn conflict and misunderstanding into opportunities for growth
creative struggle to birth the things of the Spirit by listening to the Spirit.

Greatness is the ministry to which we are all called to embody and share in and for the world:
seeing the world with the wonder, keenness, and delight of a child
laying aside our fears and needs, our jealousies and doubts
and saying yes to the possibilities we glimpse in and through each other.

For it's only in learning to live in and for each other
that we have any chance of learning something of what ordinary greatness is
and, therefore, of glimpsing something of who and what Jesus really gives to the world.

And, entirely off the record,
when Jesus had finished chiding the disciples about greatness and authority,
and teaching them about the real nature of the task,
he got up, and led them out for a stroll along the lakeside before dark. The women
present remained behind,
some to clean up and
others to begin cooking the evening meal. They
looked at each other and smiled, knowingly...
True greatness, indeed!

AUT
UMN

Luke 16:1-13

Capsella bursa-pastoris
Shepherd's Purse

"Named from the likeness of its seed to the bags worn at the waist by English country folk in centuries past."

23 Just a Couple of Hours
(Luke 16:1-13)

Scene One—Take 1
He had just a couple of hours …
And, though his wife ran about the house in a panic hastily packing up their belongings
and their children stood—confused, and crying in a corner—unsure of what was happening,
he knew exactly what he must do.
He kept his head.
He had just a couple of hours to act,
a couple of hours to save his family and salvage as much as he could of his reputation, his money, and his future.

For the boss was demanding to see the accounts and, once he'd handed over the books,
he was out of a job again.
Some whistle-blower had blown time on his double dealing and the game
(this particular game, at least)
was over.
Though, if he were shrewd and cool enough now, there'd be another opportunity soon.

So he ran with the accounts to the boss's two biggest clients and did a deal:
"Instant discount on all you owe him and we'll split the difference. That way we all win.
And can you put us up for a week or two until all the fuss dies down?"

Back at the office, he handed over the books;
but the golden handshake in his back pocket tempered his boss's stern reproof.
Along with the satisfaction he felt at having pulled the wool over his eyes.

Scene One—Take 2
He had just a couple of hours …
And, though his wife ran about the house in a panic hastily packing up their belongings
and their children stood—confused, and crying in a corner—unsure of what was happening,
he knew exactly what he must do.
He kept his head.
He had just a couple of hours to act,
a couple of hours to save his family and salvage as much as he could of his reputation, his money, and his future.

For the tax officials were demanding to see the accounts and, once he'd handed over the books,
he'd be facing a jail term.
Some whistle-blower had blown time on his double dealing and the game
(this particular game, at least)
was over.
Though, if he were shrewd and cool enough now, there'd be another opportunity soon.

So he asked his manager for the accounts and they sat down together and constructed the scam.
They did a deal with the two biggest clients.
"Reducing our income will lower our tax liability and mean there's no case to answer with the government. We'll give
a pay-back to the clients and then split the profit between us. That way we all win.
Though we'll have to lie low for a while, we'll live to fight another day."

AUT
UMN

Back at the office, he handed over the books to the tax inspectors;
but the golden handshake in his back pocket tempered their stern reproof.
Together with the satisfaction he felt at having pulled the wool over their eyes.

Scene One—Take 3
Last week at the pharmacy I
handed over my prescription. He
offered me a cheaper product which I
accepted. Then he
processed the prescription as usual. Quietly pocketing the profit.

Either way we view these scenes the message is the same.
Pulling a fast one! A harmless scam! It's win-win for everyone, surely?
Who minds if it's only system that gets screwed? And we all have a story to tell.
Haven't we all done it—or contemplated doing it— from time to time? Jesus

was a great story teller—taking his inspiration from the warp and weft of everyday life. Perhaps he'd
overheard the story in a corner of the market place,
or watched as the manager—or his boss—was paraded through the streets
towards accountability.
Perhaps the story was told him during some Sabbath meal at the tax collector's house.
Did he smile and nod with complicity, or was he the whistle-blower? Jesus

was a great story teller.
But it's a hard and demanding story that he tells.
It's not that it offers us a blue-print for our practical financial concerns.
He doesn't offer us advice, or seek to reprimand us, scare us, or scold us.
There's nothing about public or private sector, insider-dealing, or racketeering.
No clue as to whether we should reinterpret the oil and wheat of the story
as stocks and shares, off shore investments, or weapons sales.
Or see the unjust steward and his boss as involved with any particular bank or hedge-fund.

Yet the story haunts us, and leaves us feeling uncomfortable. Because,
while managing to pull a fast one may leave us with a sweet taste in our mouth,
the thought that it's we who might have been duped—the victims of a scam—leaves us very bitter.

Scene Two—Take 1.
St Peter's Chaplaincy, Manchester. Last week.
We had just a couple of hours.
We were rushing about in wild alarm, moving boxes and bags outside on to the street.
People stood about panicking and confused; not quite sure about what was happening.

We had just a couple of hours to act; a couple of hours to give away all we had:
free gifts "Welcome to Manchester—just to show we care. No strings attached." And yet
while some accepted the gift gladly, with broad smiles and deep thanks,
others imagined we were pulling a fast one;
promoting a scam that would require them to sign away their souls.
Hoodwinked, terminally entangled, exploited by religious weirdoes with an impossible doctrine and a
joyless lifestyle.

The police came by.
(Had some whistle-blower called time on our genuine generosity?) What wool could we be seeking to pull over exactly whose eyes?
Or were we just harmless eccentrics?

Scene Three—Take 1.
Holy Innocents Church. Morning Eucharist, Sunday September 23. Here and now.

We have just a couple of hours to act,
a couple of hours to save our reputation as the kind of church any right-minded person might want to go to.

For the boss is demanding to see the accounts and once we've handed over the books the game might be over.
Has some whistle-blower had blown time on our double dealing?
Is this really the kind of church that is true to the aspirations of its belief—liberal, inclusive, dynamic and outreaching? Or are we pulling a fast one
and promoting a scam?
Being the sort of church that prefers to ignore anything and anyone who might threaten our honed liturgical routines? Jesus

was a great story teller. But this is a hard and demanding story that he tells.
It's not that he offers us a blue-print for our practical missionary concerns.
He doesn't offer us advice, or seek to reprimand us, scare us, or scold us.
There's nothing about who we should passionately care about.
No clue as to whether we should reinterpret the oil and wheat of the story in any particular way. But

the possibility surely haunts us
(leaving us feeling uncomfortable)
that we might be guilty
of pulling a fast one; guilty
of short-changing those who most need to find a welcome; guilty
of ignoring those who would profit from being part of this community.
The awful possibility that we might be the unjust stewards of our Lord's estate.

Scene 4. One take only.
The pearly gates, on Judgment Day. Each of us lines up to present our accounts to the boss.
The queue is very long, but no-one is turned away! All
are welcomed in with
a smile!
Those
who had hoped to be amongst a very select few have a bitter taste in their mouths.
God has pulled a fast one—on all of us!

AUT
UMN

Mark 10:17-31

Ceratonia siliqua
Carob

24 X-rated

(Mark 10:17-31)

Fancy watching a film instead of a sermon? Shall we go to the movies?
Hush now. It's about to begin.
(But please note this is an X-rated film! People under eighteen years, or of a nervous theological disposition, should leave now.)

Act One. Scene One. Camera One. And *action!*

(A little known actor on his first shoot. No-one caught his name, but he doesn't charge much.
He stands before the star, Jesus, played by himself.
He's rehearsed his lines for hours before the mirror,
trying out different intonations, different accents, different expressions.
But, nervous now, he forgets all his best-rehearsed intentions.)

"Lord, what must I do to inherit eternal life?" he blurts. And then adlibs for effect:
"What must I do?"

Jesus smiles and opens his mouth to speak. And cut!

Act One. Scene One. Take Two. Camera Two, this time.

A flash back scene. It's the night before the sermon is delivered.
The preacher man turns in his sleep and dreams uneasily.
In his dream he sees himself standing before his Bible, and the face of Jesus rising out of its open pages.
"Lord!" He thinks.
"Lord, what must I do to inherit eternal life?"
"What must I do?"

Jesus smiles at him and opens his mouth to speak.
(The camera fades out and returns to the present time.)

Act One. Scene One. Take Three. This time Camera Three
films the faces of the congregation. They're
all extras, hired for the day. Students, mostly,
from the streets outside; and some older folks who've come in out of the cold for the free coffee at The End,
when the credits roll.

But the preacher man has them all on the edge of their seats.
They lean forward in anticipation, as prompted by the director.
"Just imagine you're eager to discover what this guy's about to tell you," he says. And
with their hastily learned method acting they do just that. They lean forward in
anticipation. Yet in the silence of their hearts they're kind of curious too.
After all, it's a film about eternal life.
"Lord, *what must we do* to inherit eternal life?" they wonder.

Jesus smiles and opens his mouth to speak. And *cut!*

Act One. Scene One. Take Four. All cameras zoom in for close ups of Jesus:

AUT
UMN

his face, his teeth,
his gestures. And a wide angle shot to fade in and catch the expectant faces of the crowd.

Jesus smiles and opens his mouth to speak. All catch their breath.

"What must you do to inherit eternal life? He answers their frowning faces:
"Go. Sell all you have and give it away to the poor. Then come and follow me."

"Go. Sell. Give it all away." The words fall like hammer blows.
"Go. Sell. Give it all away." The actor's face contorts in disbelief.
"Go. Sell. Give it all away." The preacher man is jolted from his dream into the jagged
light of day.
"Go. Sell. Give it all away." The hired extras suck in air between their teeth, making impulsive whistling noises. Even the hard-nosed director pauses to check the script, incredulously.

Go. Sell all you have and give it all away to the poor. Then come and follow me.

Jesus smiles and holds out his hand.
(The cameras keep rolling silently.
All the action, past, present, future,
and all the actors' faces and expressions are frozen:
caught in the timelessness of a proffered hand full of words.)

Jesus looked steadily at him and loved him.
Jesus looked at him and loved him.
Jesus looked and loved him.
Jesus looked.
And heaven's doors opened wide; and the whole created universe held its breath ...

In a sudden blind panic the rich young man turned around and ran away. He
fled, pushing his way out of the crowd, tumbling
past onlookers, running helter-skelter; he knew not where,
until, weak and exhausted, he crouched
behind the trunk of a carob tree and wept. And:
"pause the film. Freeze that image right there."

(Coffee break! Back on set in ten!
Matthew's screenplay has the young man ask "what good deed
must I do to have eternal life?" While Mark and Luke's versions have him ask Jesus: "What must I do to inherit eternal life?"

Perhaps these versions suggest this rich young man had already received many inheritances, knew their value, and was keen to acquire more.
Perhaps he was now looking for the gift that would guarantee his ultimate ever-lasting felicity.
Perhaps Jesus' response was just too much for him.
Perhaps the challenge of wholeness, the threat of life, was too much to ask.
Perhaps the question is not
whether or not he had—enough—faith in Jesus, but that he was not
yet sufficiently needy, not

yet at a place in his life where he was able to recognize his own lack of wholeness.
Perhaps the absence of wholeness for this man,
as for many of us today, is not just a consequence of a comfortable or an apparently virtuous life-style in itself,
but more to do with the weight of unacknowledged psychological distress that we carry about with us: low
self-esteem, negative
personal image, those destructive
feelings of unfocussed shame, inferiority, and perpetually living under a cloud
that hound us and prevent us from experiencing whatever it is that we really need
in order to be set free to flourish.
Perhaps.
Perhaps.
Perhaps. Who knows?

Perhaps, after all, he came back to Jesus after dark, or the next morning, with all his wealth converted into cash. Ready?)

"Unfreeze the film. Three, two, one: *action!*"

Jesus watches the young man run; then turns to his disciples.
He smiles and opens his mouth to speak.
"How hard it is," he said. "How hard it is for anyone to enter the kingdom of God."

"Well we've managed it. And that lad certainly had no excuse. Not with his money."
It was Peter who spoke, and with a particularly heartfelt passion.
(He was, after all, played by an elderly actor well-known for his permanent need of ready cash.)
"Think of all the good he could have done. Enough good deeds to guarantee him the top table in the heavenly halls!"

Jesus shakes his head slowly, looking Peter straight in the eye.
"You just don't get it, do you? None of you!"
He turns again and gestures to the crowd.
"The only thing that matters is how you treat each other. If you really want to find the kingdom, then start to look out for each other—because nothing else matters! Start
to really care for each other and everything else will just fall into place. Break down
the barriers that separate you from other people. Build up
communities of friendship and share
what you have. That's all there is to learn."

Jesus looks steadily at them and loves them. He turns to go.

One of the extras shouts suddenly from the crowd:
"Then is there no hope for any of us?"
The question lingers
in the evening air and is carried
away on the breeze. There is
silence. With their hastily learned method acting they lean forward in anticipation.
Jesus smiles and opens his mouth to speak ...

AUT
UMN

At his side a small child rises slowly to her feet and points away into the distance.
And, off camera, a camel is seen to squeeze itself very carefully through the eye of a needle.

Luke 17:11-19

Knautia arvensis
Field Scabious

"This common plant is named after the reputed ability of its juice to cure scabies and other skin diseases."

25 The Other Nine Lepers
(Luke 17:11-19)

Stand well back please!
Repulsive dermatological conditions coming through!
Skins diseases of all sorts!
Don't touch!
Stay well back there. Let them pass.

The poor dears—throw them a few coins, a bit of bread; a chicken leg;
the old coat that hangs on the backdoor.
Keep your distance, though! Oh! Don't they make you want to itch and scratch yourself!

Here is a sermon that might just make you want to itch and scratch
yourself! (And feel free to do so.) Scratch
your arms and legs. Scratch
your heads. Scratch
your ...
Perhaps you might even want to you scratch
your hearts and souls, and so open up a hole
in your spiritual armor. A space
to let the spirit in—and lead you who-knows-where.

Sometimes a good scratch is just what's needed!

They were obliged to shout to announce their approach.
"Here we are—stand clear."
"We're coming through."
"Have pity on us—we must have sinned somehow to end up like this."
"Why me? Why not you?"
"Have pity on us—do what you can for us—it might be you one day!"
"Have mercy on us."

If only cortisone cream had been invented.
If only some one had known about the need for Vitamin C.
If only people understood that hardly any skins diseases are contagious.
As it was, however, people believed differently.

And that made a huge impact on their lives.
Touch a leper, and their impurity sticks to you:
("Tick! Got you! Now you're impure!"
Like a children's playground game gone nightmare-mad.)
Touch a leper, and no one will touch you.
People won't touch you—for twenty-eight days and twenty-eight nights.
They won't dare!
They won't brush against you in the crowd—stand well back please!
They won't enter your house—stand well back please!
Their children won't play with yours—stand well back please!
You can't go to work, or to the well, the river, the market place, to the supermarket, to the bus stop,
the soccer match, the hairdresser's, the pub, the hospital, your local place of worship—stand well back please!

No job, no money, no social life. Shunned: even by your own family, children, partner, lover.
"For better or for worse, in sickness and in health."
But not in the case of leprosy.

They'll keep staring at you—just to check you aren't one of them.
(What's that blemish she's got on her cheek? Was it there yesterday?
What's that flaky skin on his collar? When did that start?)

A group of these poor souls is wandering through a village, begging as they go.
(Picture the scene.)
They call to Jesus and he sees them.
(It doesn't say he touched them either—he was a man of his time, after all!)
But he sends them off to the priests. For they alone can decide if, and when, anyone is healed.
They alone would decide if a miracle had happened. And then,

on the way, something did happen. On the way
their lives were changed. And not just one of them—but all ten! What
a miracle! What
a sight! (What
a relief! The relief we all experience when that blasted itch stops itching!)

Imagine the scene again.
The priests gradually come closer.
"Show yourself. Let me see that arm. Take your clothes off."
They check and double check: perfect
skin! Smooth as a baby's bottom! Well, well! Then they sound the all-clear: "God is Good!"

One of the former lepers runs home for a hot shower and a change of clothes. Oh, the bliss!
Two of them go out for a meal and a drink together, dressed just as they are.
One—a younger man—goes back home to the comforts of his wife.
Another, a market trader, rushes off to see if she still has a business.
Another, an elderly man, sits down and cries when he finds his wife has left him for some one else.
Two—middle-aged ladies—take tea and scones together in the little tea shop round the corner. (Their former weekly custom now restored.)
And the ninth one—a doctor—hurries dutifully back to his patients. All of them

are so happy to put that awful chapter of their lives behind them! All of them
intend to lead holier lives and to avoid temptation in the future.
(Just in case the disease comes back.) And all of them,
without exception,
resolve to be kinder to lepers in the future.

Yet just one of them
turns around and goes back to Jesus, lies prostrate on the ground, and says Thank You. And he
isn't Jewish. He's
an outsider. An undesirable. A
foreigner. A
person who will once again
be shunned by his former leper friends: who never talk with strangers. Ever.

25 The Other Nine Lepers

His old life would still be there for him! Cured—yes! But welcomed into the community?

Those who listened and watched Jesus that day in the village knew
that what had happened there meant one thing—
and one thing
only. That God loves everyone. That God heals everyone.
Whatever the color and condition of their skin.

And those who read and listened to Luke's gospel in the early days of the church knew
it meant one thing—and one thing only:
that in God's kingdom there are no outsiders. "Outsiders
are just as good as us. We are all the same. Equal. Whatever
the color and condition of our skin."

And those of us gathered here today?
Those of us who read and listen to Luke's gospel here. What does it mean for us?
Where's the good news for us
to hear and share today?

Jesus tells the foreigner: "Your faith has made you well." (But
weren't all ten healed already? So what
does Jesus mean? What is he getting at?
Time for another scratch of our heads, and minds, and hearts.)

What does it mean that all ten were healed, but only one
was made well? That all
ten received the free gift of healing that God gave them, but that only one
makes the connection; only one
has the imagination to connect the presence of Jesus with the breath-taking events that day;
only one
sees that Jesus serves
as a sign of something bigger than himself; something extraordinary:
a sign that God's *power for life* refuses to be defeated, overcome, or resisted,
a sign that God will not permit deathliness and fear of sickness to triumph,
a sign that God's endless, creative loving will never allow anything or anyone
to be on the outside
of God's love,
a sign that God, "who gives life to the dead and who calls into existence things that do not exist,"[10]
longs for us to let go of the things that prevent us from receiving fullness of life,
a sign that God calls us to let go of our fears and anxieties, our paranoia, and our deep insecurity,
a sign that God desires us
to say yes to life, yes to life, yes to life
to say thank you for what has been, and yes! yes! yes!
to all that will be:
to heed the gut feeling we get from time to time,
to follow the hunch, and assent to the possibility that God
will never fail us.

Say yes. Just reach out and
touch!

[10] [Rom 4:17]

Revelation 7: 2-4, 7-12; Matthew 5:1-12

Wheat

"The curious name 'Bouquet of Jerbs' derives from the French for a stook of wheat or corn, and describes the firework shape it makes against the skyline."

26 God's Fireworks

(Revelation 7:2-4, 7-12; Matthew 5:1-12)

I suppose that, for every person who comes to church today to celebrate All Saints Day,
there will be scores more attending Guy Faulkes' Day celebrations. Indeed for the past few nights there
seem to have been bonfires and fireworks everywhere.

No matter how wet the grass, damp the air or cold the wind,
huddling round a bonfire,
"ooh-ing" and "aah-ing" at fireworks,
is irresistible to most people. Though these days most have forgotten everything
about who Guy Faulkes was, and about the origins of the various elements that make up a typical
"Bonfire Night Experience."

We call it a bonfire, but it was originally a bone fire;
to burn the bones of Christians removed from church yards
to make space for future generations.

And then there are the fireworks: fascinating
in their variety; exhilarating in their effect.

Who can forget their names?
Squibs; Crackers; Thunder
Flashes; Silver
Fountains; Golden
Rain; Mines of Serpents; Bouquets of Jerbs;
Catherine Wheels; Roman Candles. They fascinate
and exhilarate: they
never fail.
The only problem you can possibly have with them is dampness:
once they're damp they're useless.

The Thunder Flashes won't flash,
Catherine Wheels won't revolve,
Roman Candles won't light.

Catherine Wheels
(after St Catherine: tied to a cartwheel and torn to pieces).

Roman Candles
(Christians dipped—still living—into tar, tied to poles, and set alight
to illuminate Nero's gardens for his guests). Oh Yes!

Catherine Wheels and Roman Candles were Christian saints.
And Christian saints—just like fireworks—
are fascinating in their variety
and exhilarating in their effect.

The Christian saints we remember today are many and varied:
known and unknown,
from every nation on earth,
of every color, shape, size, gender, and orientation.

AUT
UMN

And all of them lived lives of crackle and sparkle! They
are God's fireworks:
giving themselves utterly in the service of God;
allowing themselves to be burned up in God's service,
and consumed for his glory: lighting up the darkness around them.

Anyone can be saintly—you don't need to be a monk, nun, or priest.
Dons and doctors,
nurses and newsvendors,
students and secretaries,
mothers and miners,
and those many unknown faces who are imprisoned, tortured, murdered
just for daring to believe. Please

God, that each of us in our calling
may dare
to believe, dare
to serve, dare
to be
(as suggested by Hildegard of Bingen)
an alive and brightly burning offering
to the God who calls each of us
out of dampness
into the warmth, and generosity, and light of the kingdom.

BANG!

Isaiah 1:10-18; Luke 19:1-10

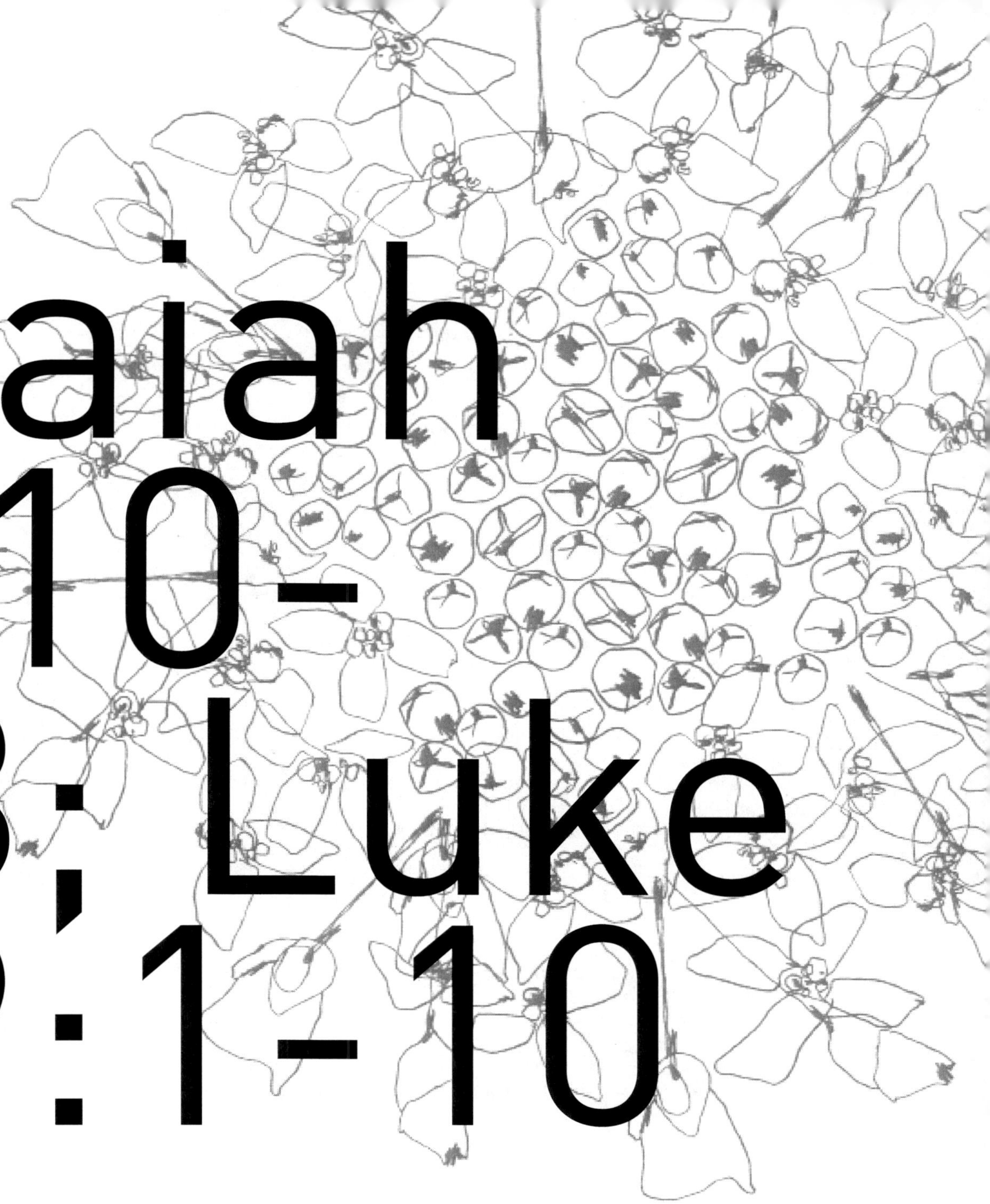

AUT
UMN

Thlaspi arvense
Field Penny-Cress

"In various European languages, this plant was named from its coin-shaped fruits."

27 The Algorithm of Salvation

(Isaiah 1:10-18; Luke 19:1-10)

Here's a sermon dedicated to mathematicians in every land.
And to the memory of Zacchaeus,
patron saint of tax collectors, revenue officials, actuarians, brokers, dealers, hedge-fund managers, bank workers, and accountants everywhere.

It's a mathematical sermon
(although no calculators are permitted as you listen).
You need to do your own reckoning up in your head as we go along
and then see whether we all arrive at the same answer.

Now that may be hard for a small fraction of us;
for in these times such arithmetical demands can divide a congregation;
added to which I have no desire in any way to subtract from your faith,
but rather, hopefully, to let God multiply it by a few percentage points.

So here's a simple well-known sum to start you off
(and get you in the mood for more complex computations later):
Question: one, plus one, plus one, equals what?

Well: here's my own working out. (See how it compares with yours.)
I am one of three brothers.
We are the sum of our parents' calculations;
the complex calculus of their aspirations.
So the answer: one, plus one, plus one, equals
three.
And together we make the triplication of the assets
that my parents wanted,
to complete the long working out of their lives.

But contrast, now, another's working out: Zacchaeus. His presence was a welcome addition—for no-one.
For his worldly increase was based on a continuous subtraction
from the poor wealth of others.

Chief tax collector was he; a rich man.
Rich enough, because of the franchisees who farmed his taxes for him round the whole region of Jericho.
Rich enough, because of the way he creamed off a percentage of everything for himself.
Rich enough, to afford the inflated Roman body guards who kept him safe.
Safe:
except for the whispers, the jeers and "fat cat" catcalls that followed him everywhere,
like annoyingly indivisible fractions.

By all accounting he was a crook;
the multiplication of his wealth achieved
in direct proportion to the mean square root of the misery he caused.

He marched around the axes of his two-dimensional world,
a tiny, diminutive figure—a small dot of a man—like
a difficult decimal point between the several large ciphers that always accompanied him. And, if his

27 The Algorithm of Salvation

monthly calculations were not equaled,
then a number of his heavy-handed guards would find the solution for him.

As problems went, he was painfully and permanently insoluble to the people of the region.
Insoluble, that is, until one day the original prime number came into town,
(expressed mathematically as 1+1+1=1; but work it out theologically for yourselves).

Jesus was fast approaching and Zacchaeus wanted to contemplate this unique figure
as it drew closer. So he climbed
a nearby tree as fast as the interest rates climb
during a sudden recession.
And, indeed, from that moment, things would never add up easily again for him.

Jesus spoke to him. There and then, his number was up!
"Zacchaeus! Zacchaeus! Come down. I'd like to eat with you."
Simple words: easy enough to reckon, perhaps;
but then
the figures and numbers, the ciphers and calculations, fell tumbling like loose change,
from Zacchaeus' deep pockets.

His rules for calculating compound interest, his treasured arithmetical and algebraic symbols
all fell away
as he heard the letters of his name spelled out. Spoken aloud. His name!

His name! Jesus was calling him by his name!
(When had anyone last done that?) Zacchaeus
came down the tree—transfigured. He came down a man.
He was made up: a fraction of his real self no longer.
He was a figure made complete: a whole man, with no inconvenient remainder. Together
they walked a few steps:
just enough for him to recognize, in Jesus, the algorithm of his salvation.

The crowd murmured and growled, like bulls and bears
squabbling in some market place or exchange hall.
All eyes were on them.
And, as they watched, some control mechanism in Zacchaeus collapsed,
like a market in free-fall.
The tariffs that protected the finances of his soul were suddenly swept away and abolished.
The artificial barriers of his false integrity disintegrated;
and his humanity leapt forth from him,
connecting—oh so profitably—
with Jesus and with the crowd around them.

This exchange was unlike anything he'd experienced in his life;
its rate caught him by surprise as, breathlessly he cried aloud,
announcing to the crowd "half my possessions to the poor
and the fourfold repayment of any claim of overcharge, overpayment, or miscalculation."

The crowd inhaled sharply and, in the brief silence that ensued,

did their own ad hoc creative accountancy in their heads. The body
guards melted swiftly away,
disappearing, like good money after bad, in a run of panic trading …

In the hours that followed, Zacchaeus watched as his gilt-edged reserves disappeared
and as his nice little pension fund evaporated
for good.
His savings were no more.
(Though he little more than suspected the real security of his future.)

So, he determined: he'd just have to start again, and find a better investment this time.
And, besides, what price his current savings, anyway:
if his futures seemed suddenly so healthy?

Today salvation had come his way: savings of a different sort.
Insider dealing of an altogether different kind now:
inner profit for his soul's security,
guaranteed by the endless reserves of God's infinitely gratuitous love
secured by the value of the stock of a certain Good Friday's trading.

Another gamble for Zacchaeus?
A risky hedge fund?
Or a gilt-edged investment: the best he'd ever know?

He went off rejoicing, to a celebration and a meal. Champagne all round!
Well, no expense spared tonight. Or in the future!

The crowd sat around and wondered.
Was there a profit in this for them also? (They did their calculations carefully.)

And what of me? And what of you?

Take time to think it through.
No pressure; no cold calling, or hard sell on the phone.
No debts to incur.
No deposits up-front.
No annoying small print or hidden financial penalties.
No complex figures to be calculated.
Just the rich risk of responding somehow—somehow, somehow—when our name is called out!

Ready?

Luke 3:7-18

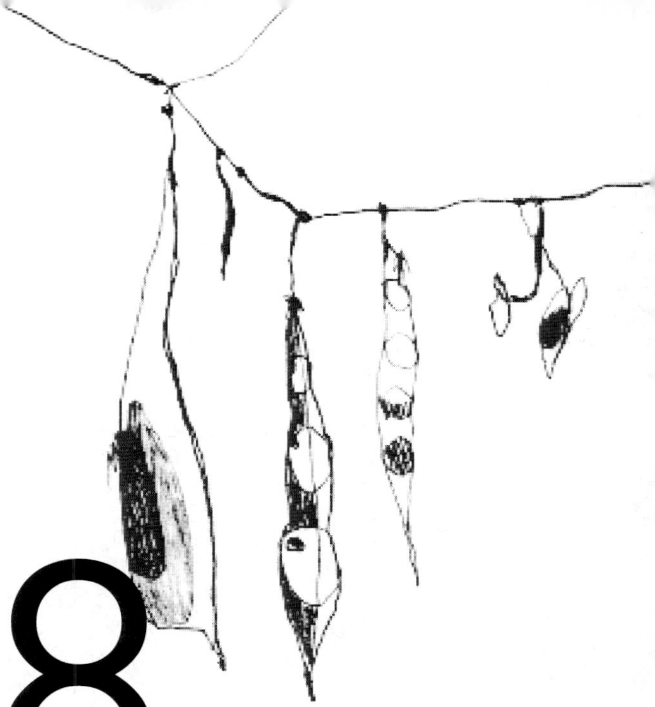

AUT
UMN

Phaseolus coccineus
Runner Bean

28 How Many Beans Make Five?
(Luke 3:7-18)

A quick quirky question for you: an Advent brain teaser to ask your friends and neighbors.
How many beans make five?

This secret-sacred wisdom was passed down to me
by my father and by his father
before him. And I do not know how many generations back I would need to go
to find who first asked the question. How many beans make five?
Do you know the answer?

My father passed the answer on to me with much fuss and ceremony, and
there I was: set up for life, with the answer to one of its more burning questions!

How many beans make five?
Mr T, my history teacher, looked around the room as he asked the question to the class.
There was stone-faced silence amongst my peers …
Reading our blank faces he bellowed again, with increased desperation and outrage,
demanding to be told the answer, as he might routinely have demanded of us the date war broke out:
how many beans make five? My

moment had come! I sensed the fateful hand of unforgettable triumph descend upon my head.
I raised my hand and answered. "Please, sir. I know."
Do you?
The answer provoked a gasp of disbelief around the room.

"This boy," said Mr T, "has more wisdom in his little finger …"
My triumph was short lived
(as was my enhanced status with Mr T, who died shortly afterwards),
but the revenge of my class mates was long-lived and, for them, delicious.
How many beans make five?
I wish I'd never known!

Sometimes life gives us extraordinary teachers. (Mr T was one of them.)
Unique, unforgettable, complete "one-offs,"
as were my father and grandfather. Bless them all!
And often the things they try to teach us are nothing
compared to the things we actually learn from them. Life can be like that, can't it?

John the Baptist was one such.
Just like my Mr T:
awkward, unkempt, unorthodox, uncomfortable to be around, and more than slightly mad.

John the Baptist was Jesus' teacher. Or—more accurately—Jesus hung around him for a while
at a formative time of his life. And

twice a year we remember John. We bring him out of storage, dust him down, and wind him up:
to put him through his paces.
In the summer he's a wanderer, dressed in camel skins, and eating locusts. An ox
of a man smelling of animals and sweat, who lost his head after a party trick went wrong.
In the winter, advent-tide, John spits

28 How Many Beans Make Five?

and swears and waves an axe about his head, threatening
to split us clean in half, straight down the middle, unless we start to mend our ways:

How many coats should you have?
How much food do you actually need?
How many locusts make five?
Hurry, hurry! For the end is nigh and time is running out.

John is uncomfortable company for us as we realize our own time is running out
in the rush to get Christmas sorted.
He screams out impossible questions that tie us in knots,
but which refuse to let us go.
How much?
How many?
Why do you do this?
Why do you want that?
What's life all about?
Tell me. Answer me. You there at the back! Raise your hand if you know.

Jesus was fascinated. What a teacher!
He hung around him for a long while and listened; following him across the desert wilderness,
and more than once finding himself on the end of John's rough and ready tongue. In fact

all the people who daily came out to run the gauntlet of his rage
felt that the radical message John had,
the difficult questions,
the unforgettable impact
(the way he really got up the noses of the leaders of his day),
singled him out as a man who could lead a revolution:
turn the known world upside down. if
he'd wanted to.

The crowds openly spoke of him as the Messiah,
but he only shook his head, and wiped the sweat off his brow with the back of his hairy hand.

The real teacher was still to come, he said.
It wasn't him—but another.
One whose legacy would not be rough words and angry gestures,
but whose stories would get under your skin and make you scratch your soul.
One who would never lose his head, but simply give his life.

John's teaching was an inspiration; but, like many teachers,
often the things he tried to teach were nothing compared to the things people actually learned from him.

Jesus' pondered John's questions,
and then knew
he had to find his own answers,
discover his own path,
go his own way, and respond to the calling that was his and his alone.

AUT
UMN

Jesus eventually left, taking with him John's passionate desire for justice,
a few of his best followers,
and a knack for asking awkward questions.
He left the wilderness to John and chose, instead, the towns, villages, and marketplaces.

Three hectic years ahead of him. (And uphill all the way!) But,
as he sat around the fires with his closest, and a cup of wine to cheer their hearts,
it was something Jesus felt he'd been born to.

He remembered the stories his mother had told him about his birth,
wondering how much was fact, and how much fond fiction.
And he cherished the things his father Joseph had taught him,
(passed down for generations on his father's side).

He remembered his teachers, their strange ways, and those endless,
curious questions in the Temple.
He remembered the sense he'd had at his baptism,
the possibility he'd sensed in his being,
the need to say yes and to assent to the calling he felt rising within him,
the need to speak out and make a difference,
to ask awkward questions and somehow find the answers.

How many beans make five?
Does it matter? I'll tell you, if you like. But you may not thank me for the answer.
Let me ask you instead, a different question.
A quick quirky question for you: an Advent brain teaser to ask your friends and neighbors.
Raise your hand if you know the answer.
Soon it's Christmas once again. And, who knows, perhaps our last ...
"What then should we do about it?"

And will our answer provoke a gasp of disbelief?

An Afterword

It was Dean Edward Patey of Liverpool who was one of those who inspired me to take risks. He preached passionately about the need to move away from "Mickey Mouse religion" and make Churches and Cathedrals places where erudition and good music could inspire people to make a difference. I remember reading his "Risk-taking God" (1991) and recognizing that the Jesus whom he spoke of was a risk taker. Being a Christian disciple and avoiding the "niceness" which Terry Biddington rightly finds so difficult, became part of my journey in ministry and still makes some of my listeners uncomfortable and maybe a little angry for stirring their still pools of faith.

I have enjoyed the challenge of reading these sermons. It has made me engage in a process of self-examination about the quality of my own preaching. Do I really "bring the congregation to an immediate and inescapable encounter with the scriptural text?" Do I bring it alive for them; "interrogate them, and entice them out of their boxes?" Have my sermons got the narrative quality that we can see emerging in this "Risk-Shaped Preaching?"

Another of my heroes, Bishop Richard Holloway, in his autobiography "Leaving Alexandria" (Canongate, 2012) writes of the struggle for truth in preaching:

"I was to become fascinated by Saint Paul's description of Christian preachers as 'deceivers yet true'. We become true deceivers when we understand the purpose of our deceptions, when we admit that the stories we tell carry their own meaning within them, even if there is no objective reality beyond them, no movie actually seen, no stone actually rolled away from the tomb. Trouble comes when we understand what's going on and start feeling guilty about it. That's when we become false deceivers. To be a true deceiver you have to believe your deception...Tell your listeners that there was no movie, no resurrection, but that the story itself has its own power to release them—try to stop deceiving them in fact—and they will turn on you."

That "the story itself has its own power to release them" is at the heart of Terry Biddington's preaching and he manages to do it without producing a congregation of listeners who become antagonized and angry. He coaxes, encourages, affirms, uses humor and the unexpected to bring stories to life and encourage a congregation on a journey with him. He uses the language of the pub, the coffee shop, and the street to communicate rather than obtuse theological clichés. He is also unafraid of the poetic, and these sermons invite you to inhabit the world of dreams as words conjure up mental pictures of a world where the beauty of God might be found amidst man's woven chaos.

These are no "cold coals." Even if we find we cannot exactly imitate Terry Biddington's style, we can learn from the way in which he tells the story. That will involve us in "Risk-Shaped Preaching" because it will challenge the hearer in a way that those First Century Galileans were challenged by the stories of that remarkable itinerant preacher Jesus of Nazareth. Then as now niceness and comfortable preaching will simply allow the Christian preacher to wander gently down "the primrose path to the everlasting bonfire." Here—in this collection—is something very different.

Bishop Stephen Lowe, April 2012